Sister Wendy Contemplates

SAINT PAUL IN ART

This book is dedicated
to dear Sister Liza Mason and Sister Gillian Leslie
who were so helpful,
and to
dear Father Stephen Blair,
to whom every word was dictated.

SISTER WENDY BECKETT

Sister Wendy contemplates

Saint Paul in Art

ST PAULS

Cover design and reprographics: DX Imaging, Watford, Herts, UK.
Cover illustration: *St Paul*, unknown mosaic artist.

Published by ST PAULS, UK

ISBN 978-0-85439-752-5

Set by Tukan DTP, Stubbington, Fareham, UK
Printed by AGAM, Cuneo, Italy

ST PAULS is an activity of the priests and brothers of the Society of St Paul who proclaim the Gospel through the media of social communication.

Contents

Introduction 7

PART ONE

1. *St Paul,* Andrea Vanni 11
2. *The Stoning of St Stephen,* Adam Elsheimer 15
3. *The Conversion of St Paul,* Michelangelo 19
4. *The Conversion of Saul*, Pieter Bruegel the Elder 23
5. *The Conversion of St Paul,* Francesco Parmigianino 27
6. *Paul Let Down in a Basket,* twelfth-century mosaic 31
7. *The Communion of the Apostles,* Andrea Bartolo 35
8. *Saul before the Proconsul,* Raphael 39
9. *St Paul Healing the Cripple at Lystra,* Karel Dujardin 43
10. *Paul and Barnabas at Lystra,* Nicolaes Berchem 47
11. *St Paul Preaching in Athens,* Raphael 51
12. *St Paul Preaching at Ephesus,* Eustache Le Sueur 55
13. *St Paul on Malta,* Adam Elsheimer 59
14. *St Paul with the Viper,* wall painting in Canterbury Cathedral 63
15. *Miracles of St Paul*, early fifth-century ivory diptych 67
16. *St Paul in Prison,* Rembrandt 71
17. *St Paul Sends the Letter to the Ephesians*, miniature 75
18. *St Paul,* Aidan Hart 79
19. *Sarcophagus of Junius Bassus*, detail 83
20. *The Beheading of St Paul,* Alessandro Algardi 87
21. *The Ecstasy of St Paul,* Nicolas Poussin 91
22. *St Paul Enthroned,* Domenico Beccafumi 95

PART TWO

23. *St Paul,* artist unknown 101

24. *St Paul,* Andrea Di Bartolo 105

25. *St Paul,* El Greco 109

26. *St Paul,* Georges de la Tour 113

27. *St Paul,* Masaccio 117

28. *St Paul,* Andrei Rublev 121

29. *St Paul,* Theophanes the Greek 125

30. *The Apostle Paul,* Dionysius 129

31. *The Virgin and Child with Saints Paul and Jerome,* Bartolomeo Vivarini 133

32. *St Paul at His Desk,* Tournier or Valentin 137

33. *St Paul,* attributed to the Master of the Pala Sforzesca 141

34. *St Paul Writing,* Pier Francesco Sacchi 145

35. *An Elderly Man as St Paul,* Rembrandt 149

36. *St Paul Seated Reading,* after Jacob de Gheyn III 153

37. *Saints Peter and Paul,* Carlo Crivelli 157

38. *The Virgin and Child with St Peter and St Paul,* workshop of Dirk Bouts 161

39. *Twelfth-century Fresco* 165

40. *Statuette of St Paul*, late fourth century 169

Acknowledgements 173

Introduction

Of all the gifts God has given His Church, none is greater than the theological quality of the four Evangelists. The Gospels were written by men with a profound capacity to understand the meaning of Jesus. Yet they were matched, some might think even surpassed, by the theological greatness of St Paul. All that we have come to understand about Our Blessed Lord has its origin in the Gospels and the Epistles. Every Doctor of the Church (St Augustine, St Thomas Aquinas) has pondered intently upon this unique revelation of God: pondered it, prayed their way into it, ordered and reordered it. To know "Jesus Christ and Him crucified" was the hard-won privilege of St Paul, and one that he offers to us in his Epistles. If you too want "to have the mind of Christ", then it is in St Paul's letters, approached humbly and seriously, that you will find it. He is the only writer of the New Testament whom we can know personally. St Luke tells us something of his life in the Acts of the Apostles, but we can know his very heart in his actual words from his letters. Every writer in the New Testament reveals Jesus to us, but I always think there is a special power in the revelation of St Paul, perhaps because his struggles "to comprehend, even as I am comprehended", are so visible.

Theologians believe that St Paul was probably born between the years 7-10 AD. Pope Benedict XVI, himself a theologian, and so by definition a man who values St Paul, has officially declared a special Jubilee Year to celebrate the two-thousandth anniversary of his birth. It will be a "Pauline Year, beginning on 28 June 2008 and ending on the 29 June 2009". The Pope hopes that there will be "study conventions and special publications on Pauline texts… to make ever more widely known the immense wealth of the teaching they contain". We enter into the grace of this Pauline Year, not only by reading about St Paul, but far more, by actually reading St Paul himself. The trouble is, of course, that it is impossible to "read" St Paul in the accepted sense. His text is too dense, its power too deep to be comprehended, except word by word. Saints have lived their lives on a single phrase of St Paul. I think lovingly of St Elizabeth of the Trinity, that young French nun, whose short life in Carmel was transformed by three small words in St Paul's Letter to the Ephesians. She liked to quote it in Latin "*ad laudem gloriae*", to the praise of His glory, and she set herself to become precisely that, a living "praise of His glory". When we read of the terrifying non-experience of God that Mother Teresa of Calcutta relates with tears of anguish, we are reading about what it means to live what St Paul wrote to the Corinthians, that God has made Jesus "our sanctification". Think what this means, to have no sanctification, no holiness of your own. Quite unconsciously, one could even say innocently, we need the comfort of feeling that we serve God, love God and pray to God. But if Jesus is our holiness, and we have none of our own, nothing human on which to rely, then we will know the dereliction in which there is no space for anything but Jesus. Mother Teresa lived this out: Jesus was, indeed, her "holiness". If we knew the secrets of the saints, we might well find similar phrases from St Paul that explain the absoluteness of their surrender in love. "I live, now, not I, but Christ lives in me." This is what it means to be holy and St Paul assures us that we are all called to be "saints".

Unfortunately, artists in general have not been all that taken by St Paul. His life contained at least two dramatic moments, his conversion and his martyrdom, but for some reason his complex personality has not attracted the attention one would expect. There are hundreds of pictures of St Jerome, and of St Mary Magdalene, St George, St Sebastian, but not all that many of dear St Paul. Here though, is a selection of what seem to me the finest and most insightful, so that we can enjoy the art as art as well as a signifier of some spiritual truth. The book falls roughly into two parts, the first showing painting and sculpture that illustrates St Paul's life, while the second concentrates on his personality. Writing it has been a grace for me, and I pray "to the giver of all good gifts" that reading it will be a grace for you.

Saint Paul in Art

Part One

1.
St Paul

by Andrea Vanni
Italian, 1390s
Museum of Fine Arts, Boston.

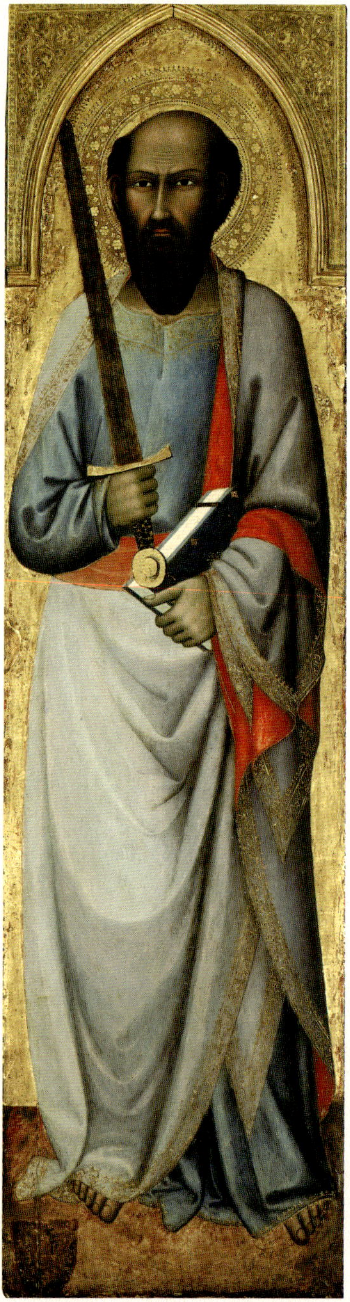

1. ST PAUL
Andrea Vanni

1. St Paul

Andrea Vanni

This is not one of the major paintings of St Paul, but it seems to me a perfect example of how the faithful have seen him over the centuries. The artist, Andrea Vanni, who was active in 1353 and died in 1413, is not considered important enough to appear in the Penguin Dictionary of Art and Artists, and the museum that owns this work, (the Museum of Fine Arts in Boston) keeps it in its storeroom. But this is one of the great museums of the world, with not enough wall space for its paintings, and many a smaller museum would hang Vanni's St Paul with pride.

At the very beginning of Christian art, St Paul was depicted as a thin man with a high forehead and balding head. He has a short, dark beard which continues upward well past his ears on either side, and his expression is rather dour. The bald head and dark beard are often enough to tell us this is St Paul, but also he holds two attributes, which Vanni shows very clearly: the sword and the book. The sword is generally taken as referring to the way Paul died: he was decapitated by a Roman executioner. In the legend, his head bounced three times and gave rise to three fountains, hence *tre fontane* in Rome, the alleged site of his martyrdom. It also seems to me to remind us of what he wrote about "the sword of the spirit". No saint has ever wielded that sword with more passion and accuracy than this heroic "Apostle of the Gentiles". His life was a continual battle.

The book refers, of course, to his epistles, the earliest in time of all the books of the New Testament. He was writing to his converts within the lifetime of those who had known Our Blessed Lord. Here too, I see another significance, because Paul had a profound knowledge and love of another book, the Old Testament. He treasured it and lived by it, and all he wrote was suffused by his reverence for God's earlier revelation.

Vanni shows Paul as humbly barefoot, and as looking out not at us but past us. He is tense, severe, impressive. We get the sense of a man whose energies are set on an all-consuming service. This is a St Paul who had no time for himself, no ambition except to forward the Word of God, no private life, no soft places. He himself is like a sword, straight and upright, ready for God's Hand. Perhaps he is like a book too, which God has written to tell us about the ineffable grace of Jesus Christ His Son. It may be, for all its charm, a rather one-dimensional picture of St Paul, but all the fundamentals are here. This is a man for whom "to live is Christ and to die is gain".

2.
The Stoning of St Stephen

by Adam Elsheimer (1578-1610), 1603-1604,
The National Gallery of Scotland.

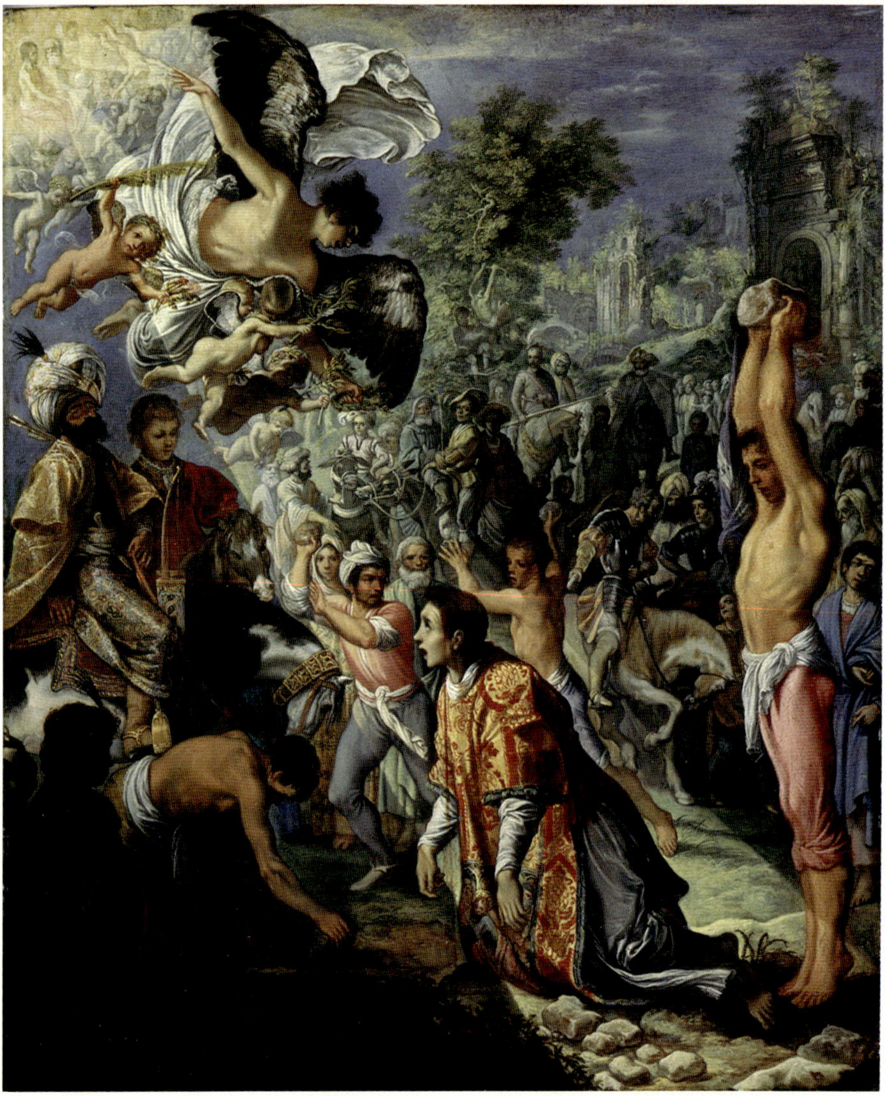

2. THE STONING OF ST STEPHEN
Adam Elsheimer

2. The Stoning of St Stephen

Adam Elsheimer

The great Rubens was deeply distressed by the early death of Elsheimer (he was only 32 when he died) and this extraordinary work on copper makes us understand why his contemporaries so valued him. St Stephen, the first martyr, radiant in his deacon's tunic, falls on his knees before the arrogant contempt of the Jewish establishment and awaits with the certainty of faith, his imminent death from stoning. He has been dragged outside the city of Jerusalem as a heretic and blasphemer, solely because of his faith in Jesus. Elsheimer seems to see the world from Stephen's viewpoint, as he prepares to die. Everything is dim and far away, except for his "judges" looking down at him from the superiority of their horses, the muscular young men stripped for their terrible activity, the angel who points upwards where Stephen "full of the Holy Spirit gazed into Heaven and saw the glory of God and Jesus standing at the right hand of God". There is a chilling contrast between this central group of six men set on the death of one man, a young innocent man at that, who, though dying, is set on eternal life, and the radiant, heavenly activity that validates his faith.

But there is an even more chilling contrast still. The lower left of the painting is dark and there we see outlined the figure of a young man who guards the clothes of the half-naked executioners. St Luke tells us that this young man consented to Stephen's death, and some scholars feel that his position as one "at whose feet the clothes were laid" suggests that he played a significant part in the terrible verdict. He was not a casual bystander, he was deeply involved. This man who glories in seeing Stephen battered into death is Saul, who we know as St Paul, here making a totally negative appearance in the Acts of the Apostles.

The genius of Elsheimer shows him in all his dark anger. Those who fear that early sins may block their way to God can take great comfort from this violent, loveless Saul.

If such a persecutor of the faith could become its most passionate defender, then there is hope for all of us. We could say that in this picture St Paul is present by his absence. He is almost an empty space, waiting to be filled with the grace of God. The absoluteness of our need for God, which Paul preached day in and day out, was something he knew from within.

3.
The Conversion of St Paul

by Caravaggio (1573-1610), 1600-1601,
Santa Maria del Popolo, Rome.

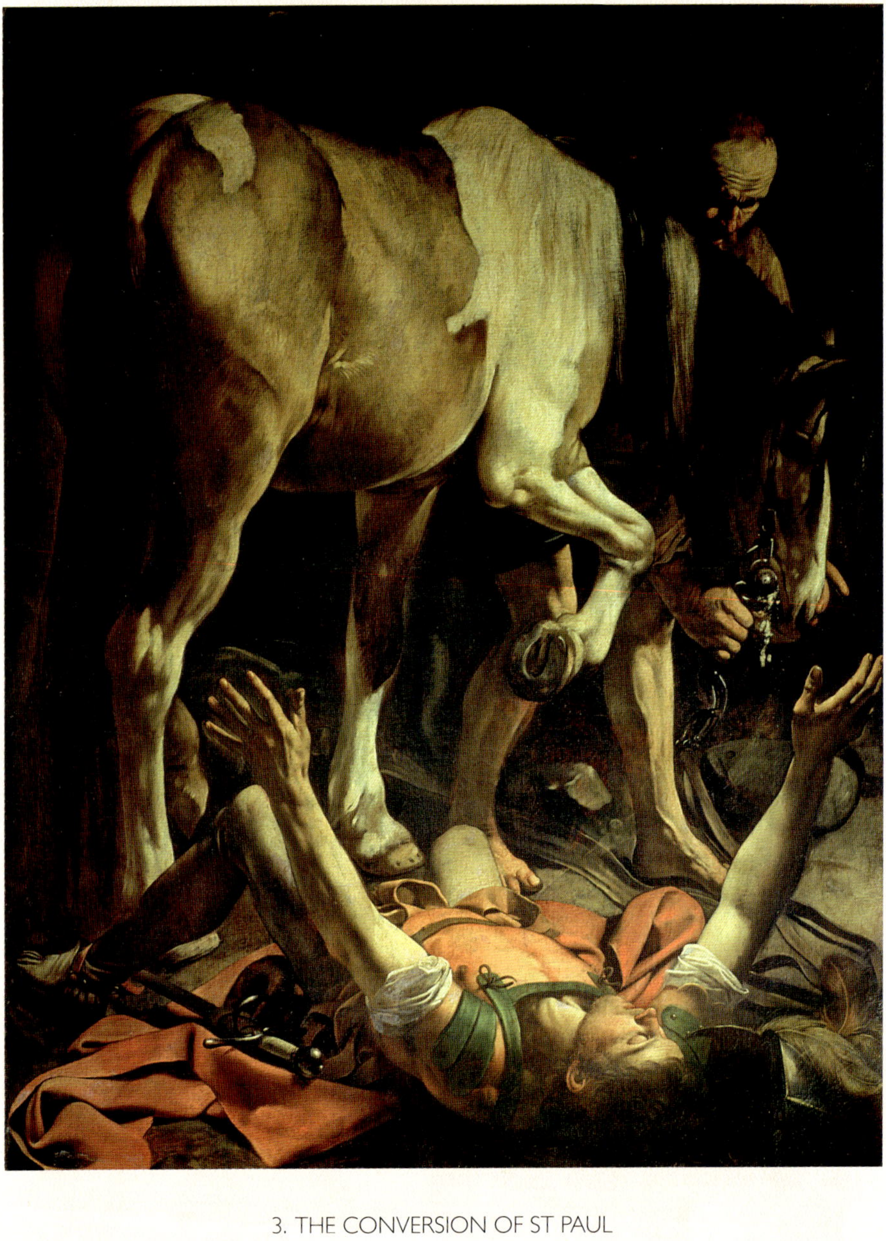

3. THE CONVERSION OF ST PAUL
Caravaggio

3. The Conversion of St Paul

Caravaggio

On the whole, artists were not especially interested in St Paul. The one event though that did attract artistic attention was his dramatic conversion. St Luke describes vividly in the Acts of the Apostles how he fell to the ground while he was on his way to Damascus "breathing threats and murder against the disciples of the Lord". Nobody could have better appreciated this all-consuming anger than Caravaggio, perhaps the most violent artist in history. I sometimes think, equally, that no artist might have so longed to be overthrown, turned from his headlong career into savagery, and brought to his senses as St Paul was. Caravaggio enters fully into the shock of this incident but maybe his fellow feeling is almost envious.

This was the central event of Paul's life, "a conversion" that changed him completely, but which poor, angry Caravaggio was never to know. He shows us St Paul, or rather, not yet St Paul but still the hostile Saul, flung from the security and eminence of his horse. Saul's head almost juts out into our space; he is upside down, dislocated, we cannot see his facial expression, but must read the whole story from his body language. A bright light is shining full upon him, blinding him, and he hears the voice of Jesus: "Saul, Saul, why do you persecute me?" All Saul can stutter in reply is, "Who are you Lord?" The heavenly answer must have chilled him to the bone. His use of the word "Lord" means that Saul understood well that it was God who was speaking to him. And God says, "I am Jesus who you are persecuting."

St Paul was to spend his life unravelling the depth of that reply. How many of us understand it? All he had done against the Christians in Jerusalem, Jesus saw as done against himself. Years later, in the Gospels, it would be remembered "whatever you do to the least of my brethren you do to me". This was something Jesus tried again and again to teach His Apostles. St Paul, "last of the Apostles, an Apostle born out of due time" may well have been the first to understand to the full the impact of this teaching. He had not consciously persecuted anyone but those who he thought were enemies of God. But to persecute is an act wholly alien to God's love. St Paul was to learn from this shattering experience that our neighbour, any neighbour, the most obnoxious neighbour, is still Jesus. Caravaggio dwells upon Paul's horror and abasement. The very horse seems to withdraw from him; notice that uplifted hoof, and his companion looks down on him in sad amazement. But those arms, outstretched in fear and astonishment, are also outstretched in surrender. It never enters Paul's mind but to obey the vision and change his entire lifestyle.

4.
The Conversion of Saul

by Pieter Bruegel the Elder (c.1530-1569), 1567,
Kunsthistorisches Museum, Vienna.

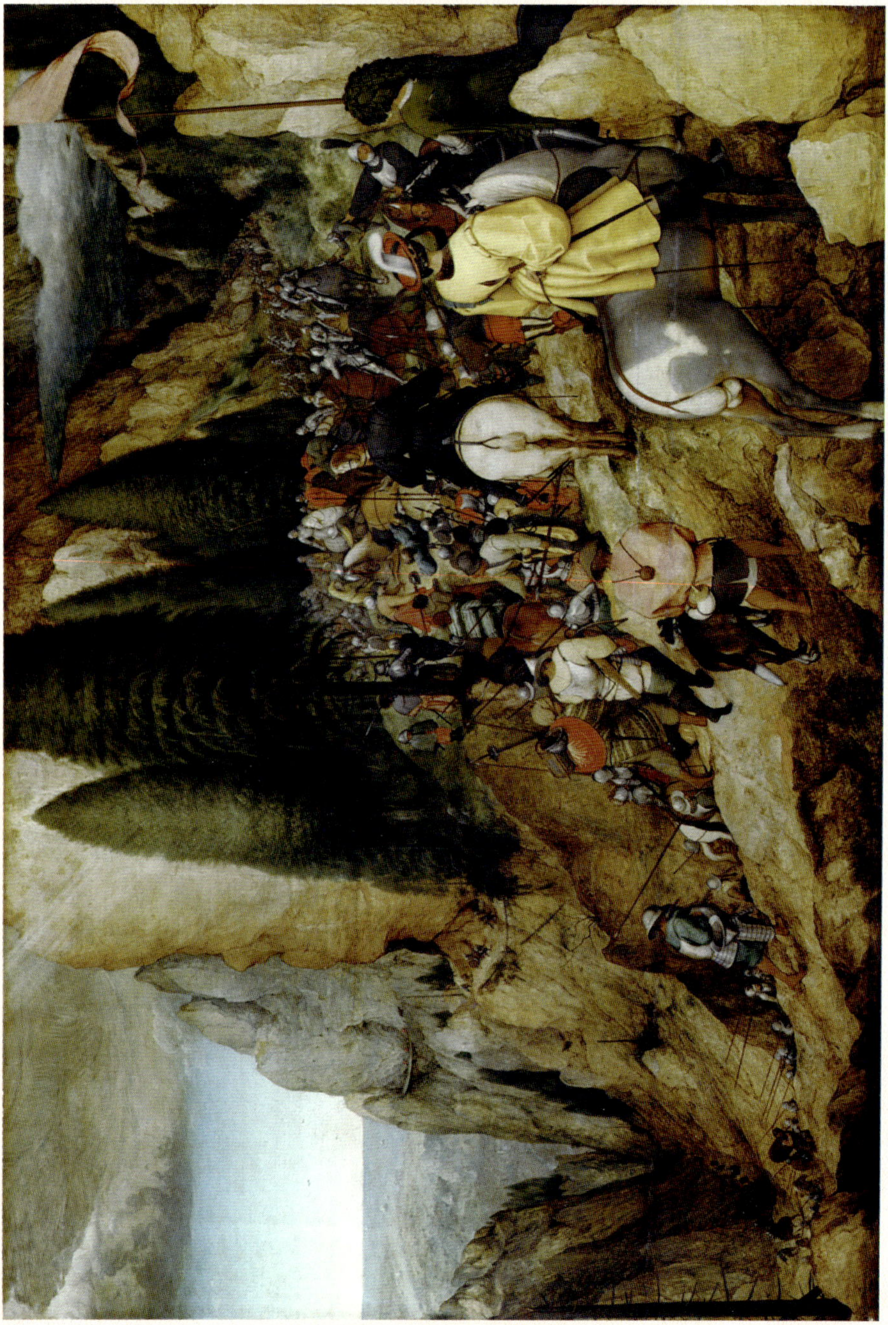

4. THE CONVERSION OF SAUL
Pieter Bruegel the Elder

4. The Conversion of Saul

Pieter Bruegel the Elder

Bruegel has an unusual gift for showing how little the world notices the central truths of our faith. He shows Jesus on the way to Calvary almost indistinguishable from the crowd of sightseers and attendants who throng the way. Mary, his mother, sees him, but we have to peer. He uses the same powerful technique when he paints the conversion of Saul. Here is a great throng of travellers, winding through the mountains, as they pass from Jerusalem to Damascus. Almost unseen among the bustle and stress of the journey is one solitary Jew falling from his horse. Hardly anyone notices. Yet Saul is encountering the living Jesus, is being forced, almost violently, to understand that his rejection of Christianity is a rejection of God, and that an unknown future awaits him. As he lies on his back, Jesus rouses him. He is not allowed to stay motionless in his humiliation and fear, but he is given a precise command, "Rise and enter the city, and you will be told what you are to do."

St Luke tells us that "the men who were travelling with him stood speechless, hearing the voice but seeing no one." Bruegel, however, imagines that there were very few who were "speechless" and that this central event that would lead to the spread of the Faith to the utmost ends of the earth, was central only for those who have eyes to see. And I also warm to Bruegel's setting. Those steep cliffs and towering rocks, with little vegetation to soften and adorn the pathway, are a good symbol of what lies ahead for humiliated Saul. From now on his life will be one far removed from those pleasant undemanding lowlands that we can see on the left. Paul is being summoned to the heights, where it will be difficult to breathe and where every step forward is arduous.

Never again will he merely be one of a multitude. When he reaches Damascus, he will find Ananias, to whom God has revealed that Paul "is a chosen instrument of mine to carry my name before the gentiles and kings and the sons of Israel; for I will show him how much he must suffer for the sake of my name." All this lies ahead of the stricken and wondering Saul but, somehow, Bruegel, that great artist, suggests it in the very landscape. This is a heedless, anxious world which needs the light of the holy Name and in which the chosen Apostle will, indeed, find much to suffer. There is bright sky behind him, there is dark sky ahead, yet we know, as Paul is to know, that in that darkness he will find the God who is "all in all".

5.
The Conversion of St Paul

by Francesco Parmigianino (1503-1540), c.1527
Kunsthistorisches Museum, Vienna.

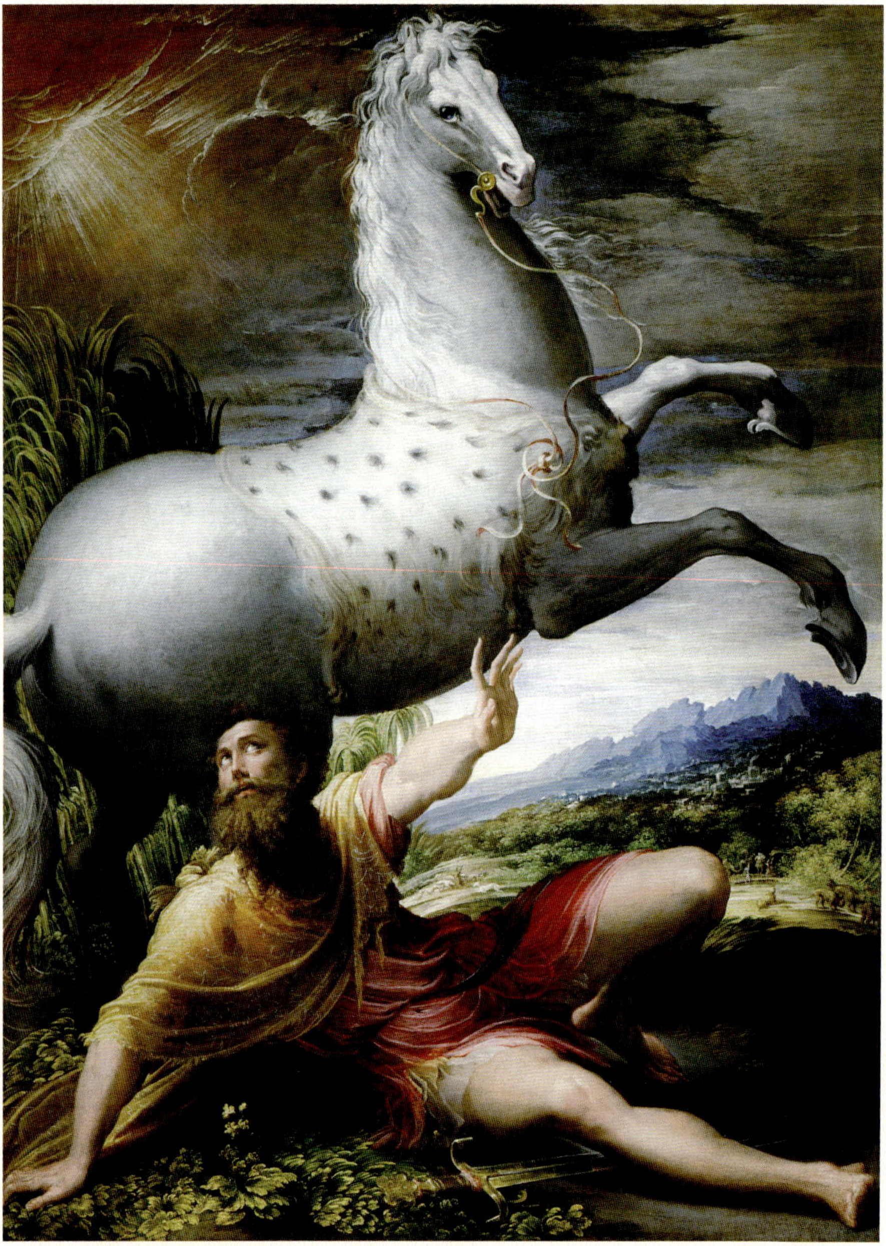

5. THE CONVERSION OF ST PAUL
Francesco Parmigianino

5. The Conversion of St Paul

Francesco Parmigianino

Saint Luke so understood the significance of St Paul's conversion that he tells the story three times in the Acts of the Apostles. St Paul tells it too, in his Epistles. This, after all, was the crucial event of his life which completely changed the direction of his journey, transforming him "from an enemy of the Cross of Christ to its great Apostle". This was how he became an Apostle, and whenever he writes to his converts he can only explain "his authority" by this encounter with the risen Jesus and the sacred commission given to him. "For I would have you know, brethren, that the Gospel that was preached by me is not man's gospel. For I did not receive it from man, nor was I taught it, but it came through a revelation of Jesus Christ. For you have heard of my former life in Judaism, how I persecuted the Church of God violently and tried to destroy it… but… he who set me apart before I was born, and had called me through his grace, was pleased to reveal His Son to me, in order that I might preach Him among the gentiles."

What distinguishes Parmigianino's majestic picture is the wonderful horse towering in animal splendour above the stricken human and the artist's poignant depiction of Paul's blindness. The ironic effect of spiritual enlightenment, which is the essence of all conversion, was physical blindness. The light from heaven took away Paul's sight. We are told "he could see nothing; so they led him by the hand and brought him into Damascus." Somehow Parmigianino makes us aware that Paul sees spiritually, and is overwhelmed by it, to the extent that he can "see" nothing else. The light of God has completely taken possession of him.

That great dappled grey, surely one of the most splendid horses ever painted, sees well enough because the blinding revelation is completely remote from all that is animal. The truth of God should illuminate everything that we see, but when we first encounter its dazzling purity we may be blind to all else. Here St Paul is even shown as semi-naked, as if the sheer impact of the presence of Jesus has stripped him of his clothes as well as his dignity and his pride. Blind Saul is frightened. He feels lost in a strange world that he cannot understand or control. But he accepts that it is Jesus who has spoken, Jesus who is Lord, and is ready to rise up and be led, humbly, toward the next stage of his journey.

6.
St Paul Let Down in a Basket

Twelfth-century mosaic,
Monreale, Palermo.

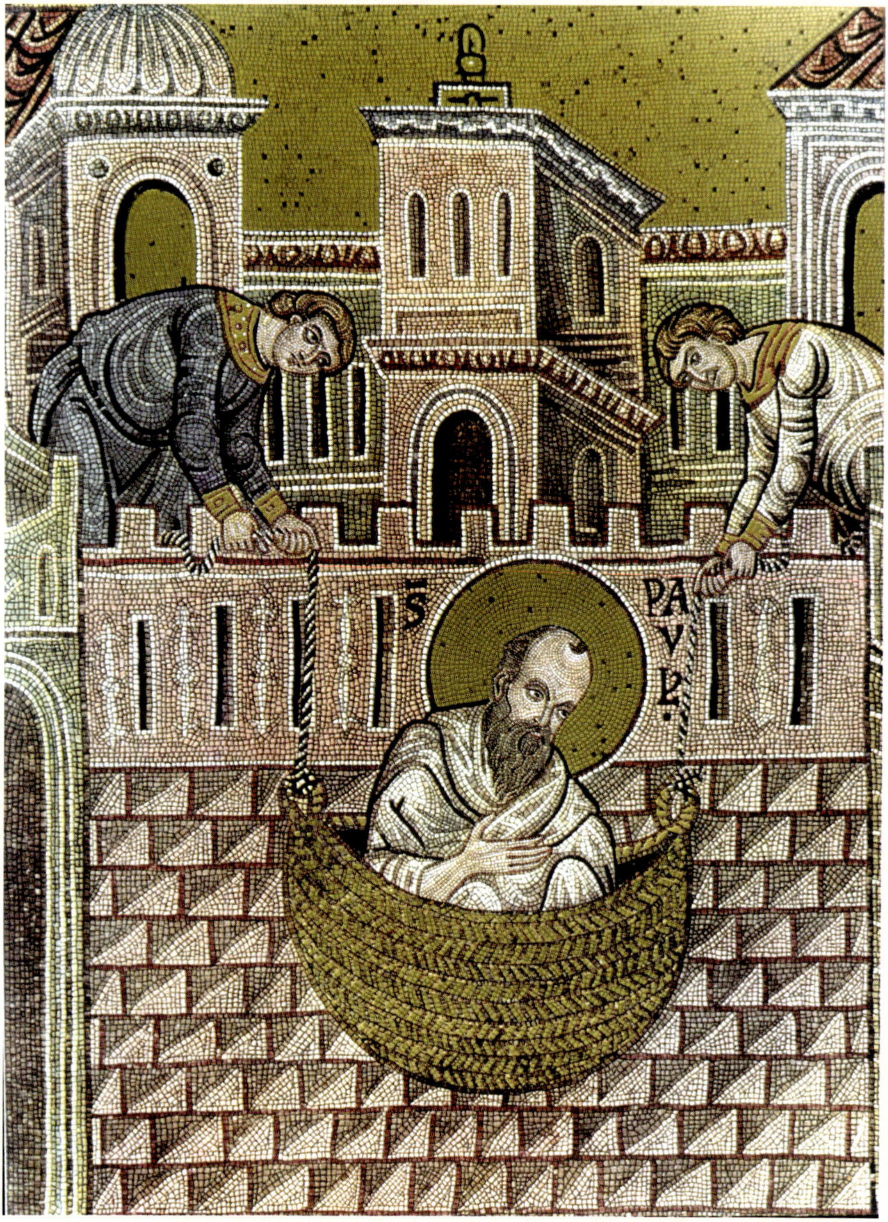

6. ST PAUL LET DOWN IN A BASKET
Twelfth-century mosaic, Monreale, Palermo.

6. St Paul Let Down in a Basket

Twelfth-century mosaic

Saint Paul reached Damascus in humiliation, blinded, led by another, and he left it in humiliation too, let down by a basket from the city walls. He had been miraculously cured by a fellow Christian, Ananias, although the immediate reaction of poor Ananias was to have nothing to do with this persecutor. Nevertheless, the Lord appeared to him in a vision and sent him to heal St Paul. "Laying his hands on him he said, 'brother Saul, the Lord Jesus who appeared to you on the road by which you came, has sent me that you may regain your sight and be filled with the Holy Spirit.' And immediately something like scales fell from his eyes and he regained his sight. Then he rose and was baptised, and took food" (he had neither "eaten nor drunk for three days") "and was strengthened".

After such a traumatic experience, such an ecstatic encounter with the risen Jesus, most of us would want silence and solitude, even if only to come to terms with what had happened. St Paul, on the contrary, was energised by the glory of the revelation. He seems to have been an extraordinarily energetic man, maybe even hyperactive. Although he tells us in his Epistles that the aftermath of his Damascus experience was meditation in the Arabian Desert ("I went away into Arabia and again I returned to Damascus. Then after three years I went up to Jerusalem"), the immediate aftermath was a most ardent Damascus apostolate. "Immediately in the synagogues, he proclaimed Jesus saying, 'He is the Son of God'. And all who heard him were amazed." The amazement was because of Paul's reputation as a fire-breathing fanatic, widely known to have come to the city only to persecute the Christians. Paul had to live down this reputation, all too well deserved, and to prove himself as one who had understood that he was one of "the servants of Christ and stewards of the mysteries of God". St Luke tells us that the more his hearers doubted him the more "he increased in strength, and confounded the Jews who lived in Damascus by proving that Jesus was the Christ". The irony was, of course, that the local Jews duplicated St Paul's own early career. He had been determined to destroy this new faith by killing those who preached it. Now he was the preacher, and fervent Jews were the persecutors. A plot was made to kill him, (much as he had plotted to kill Stephen) and the city gates were watched day and night in case he should escape. "His disciples took him by night and let him down over the wall, lowering him in a basket." This was hardly a dignified exit from the scene of his first apostolate.

This twelfth-century mosaic shows him sitting huddled up in the basket. It is quite clearly St Paul with his bald forehead and darkish beard, though the artist cannot refrain from interrupting that great dome of forehead with a little kiss-curl. The point is that St Paul is completely passive. This is not a heroic escape. He is being smuggled out through the kindness of local believers and he must have landed on the earth with a sad sense of inadequacy. The believers are at home in their lofty and elegant city. There is no home for Paul. He is cast out, like Moses in the bullrushes, cast adrift to find a city and a place for himself. There would never be an earthly city for St Paul. Even when he came to Jerusalem and "he attempted to join the disciples… they were all afraid of him for they did not believe he was a disciple." They did accept him in the end, but there was never a place where Paul could feel at home. Always the Spirit of Jesus drove him on, seeking to share the inconceivable riches of faith in Jesus. He became homeless and a wanderer for the sake of the Gospel. "Woe to me if I do not proclaim the Gospel." "I have become all things to all men, that I might by all means save some. I do it all for the sake of the Gospel, that I may share in its blessings."

This mosaic with the saint slumped in his basket, his head bent, his hand open, somehow suggests a dawning awareness that his life will be a lonely one, without status or dignity or settled home. From now on it will be only Jesus who matters "who, by the power at work within us, is able to do far more abundantly than all that we ask or think, to Him be glory".

7.
The Communion of the Apostles

Wall painting, detail, by Andrea Bartolo,
Church of the Holy Cross,
Platanistasa, Cyprus.

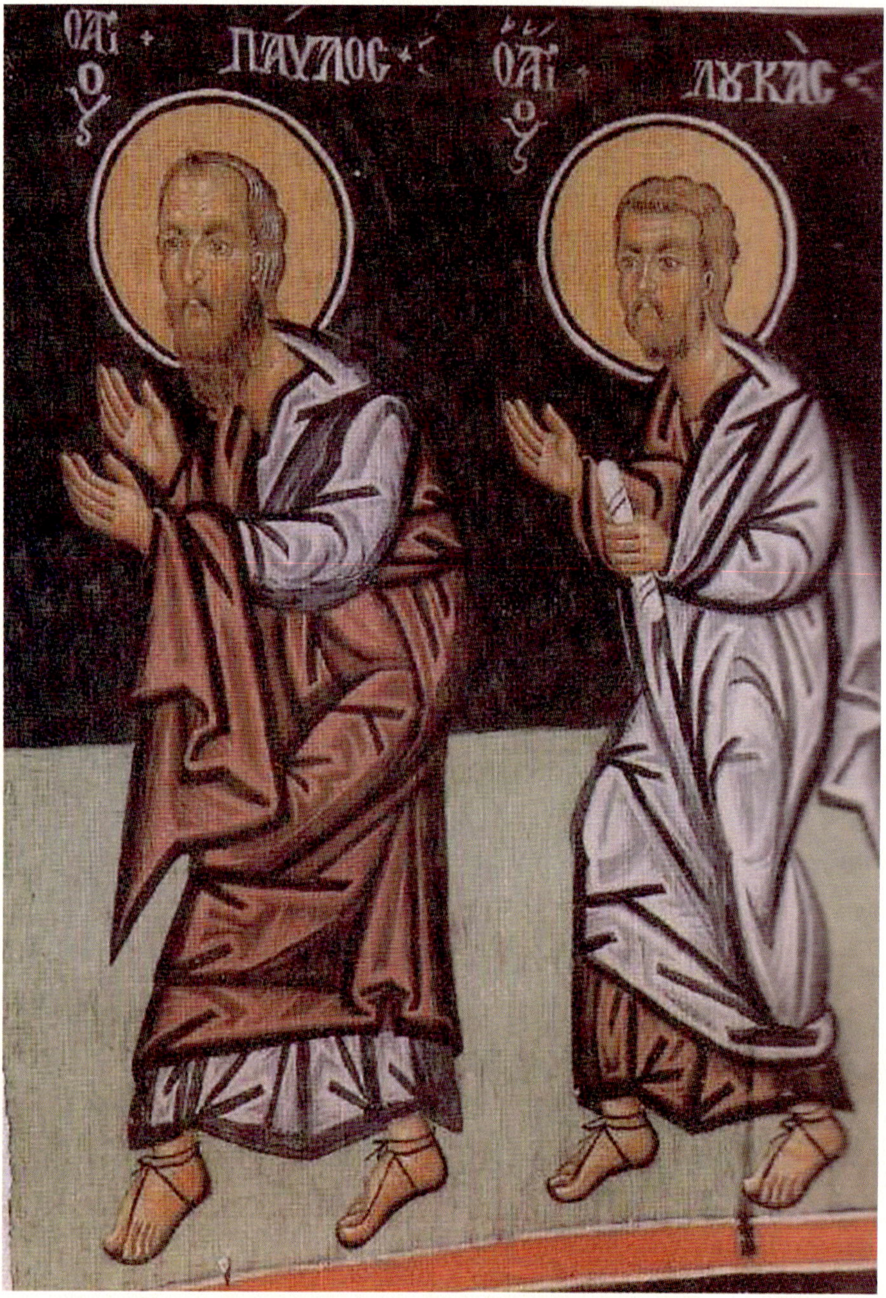

7. THE COMMUNION OF THE APOSTLES WALL PAINTING, DETAIL
Andrea Bartolo

7. The Communion of the Apostles

Andrea Bartolo

Many of us will remember religious instruction classes, or Sunday School lessons in which we trace the journeys of St Paul. There were three of them and he always had a companion. His first companion was Barnabas. "In the church at Antioch… while they were worshipping the Lord and fasting, the Holy Spirit said, 'set apart for me Barnabas and Saul for the work for which I have called them.' Then after fasting and praying they laid their hands on them and sent them off." It would not take long before it was not "Barnabas and Saul, but Saul and Barnabas", as it gradually became clear that Paul's charisma was God's unique gift to the Church. When Barnabas leaves Paul, and Mark too, they seem to be replaced by Luke, as if St Paul, aflame with the Gospel, always needed a companion.

This medieval wall painting in Cyprus commemorates this companionship. Here is St Paul, balding and bearded, moving forward with hands out-spread to embrace whoever comes his way, "Jew or gentile, slave or free, male or female". His body curves in welcome as he advances into the unknown. Behind him comes his companion St Luke. St Luke who wrote the Acts of the Apostles, never formally introduces himself, but whenever we come to a "we" passage, we assume he was present. St Paul refers to him in an Epistle as "Luke the beloved physician". Since we know that St Paul had some mysterious disease "a thorn in the flesh, a messenger of Satan to harass me", and speaks elsewhere of physical weakness, a doctor companion must have been a great blessing.

Bartolo (about whom we know very little) shows St Luke as younger than St Paul, less bowed by anxiety for the churches but following faithfully in his footsteps. He clutches firmly the manuscript which will become the Acts of the Apostles. Very subtly, their friendship is indicated by the colours of their garments: St Paul has a white tunic with a russet cloak, and St Luke has a russet tunic with a white cloak. Luke's hand, though smaller and less powerful, echoes the searching gesture of his leader. In his own lesser way, he is there to protect and support and re-echo all that this Apostle to the Gentiles has been chosen to achieve. Not even St Paul, who comes across as an essentially lonely man, worked alone. The "Communion of the Apostles" was a reality from the very beginning. Without Barnabas and Mark and Luke and all the other names St Paul commemorates so lovingly at the end of his Epistles, the great work might have faltered. St Paul preached Jesus within "a cloud of witnesses".

8.
Saul before the Proconsul

by Raphael (1483-1520), c.1515-1516,
Cartoon for Tapestry,
Victoria and Albert Museum, London.

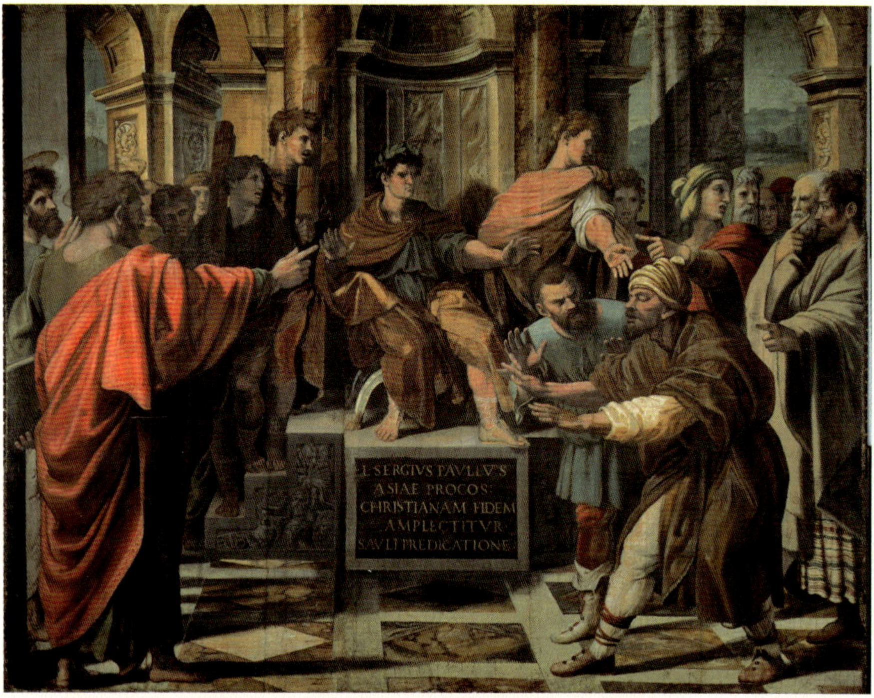

8. SAUL BEFORE THE PROCONSUL
Raphael

8. Saul before the Proconsul

Raphael

Raphael, with Michelangelo and Leonardo, is one of great masters of Renaissance painting, and his commission to design tapestries for the Sistine Chapel was as prestigious an undertaking – almost – as Michelangelo's extraordinary ceiling. Of the original cartoons from which the weavers would work, seven still survive and provide a fascinating insight into Raphael's mind and art. There are two scenes which deal with St Paul, and they are not the usual "Conversion" or the other topic that interested artists, "Decapitation".

Raphael has chosen a rather obscure incident from St Paul's first missionary journey when he and Barnabas preached the word of God in Cyprus. Here he had a disturbing encounter with "a certain magician, a Jewish false prophet, named Bar-Jesus". The magician's name is enough to make us pause and St Luke is quick to give us another name "Elymas, the Magician". The Roman proconsul "Sergius Paulus, a man of intelligence" is apparently not intelligent enough to be wary of false prophets. This man seems to have some accredited role in the proconsular court, and when Sergius Paulus summons Barnabas and Saul, eager "to hear the word of God" Elymas attacks them verbally "seeking to turn away the proconsul from the faith". He little knows with whom he is dealing. "Saul, who was also called Paul," (and from now on St Luke will give him his Christian name) "filled with the Holy Spirit, looked intently at him and said, 'You son of the devil… will you not stop making crooked the straight paths of the Lord?'" It was no small thing to be looked at intently by St Paul, and obviously he is playing with the name "Bar-Jesus", which is Hebrew for Son of Jesus. For Paul he is "son of the devil" because he is blocking the proconsul's way to understanding the truth of God.

Paul follows up his denunciation by a terrifying activity: he blinds Elymas. “Behold, the hand of the Lord is upon you, and you shall be blind and unable to see the sun for a time.” This is, of course, an eerie repetition of St Paul’s own blinding by the light of God. “Immediately mist and darkness fell upon him and he went about seeking people to lead him by the hand”, just as Paul had done on the way to Damascus.

Raphael draws us into the full drama of the scene, Paul stern with holy indignation on one side and Elymas blinded and completely bewildered on the other. St Luke tells us that “the proconsul believed when he saw what had occurred, for he was astonished at the teaching of the Lord.” As Raphael sees it, there is nothing vindictive or cruel here. Elymas, or Bar-Jesus, is blinded only “for a time” and one hopes that he, like Paul, will learn from this encounter with the living God. Meanwhile, the rather tough-faced Sergius Paulus, has understood that what Paul is teaching, the Gospel in all its wonder, is true: a miracle and a conversion.

9.
St Paul Healing the Cripple at Lystra

by Karel Dujardin (1626-1678), 1663
Rijks Museum, Amsterdam.

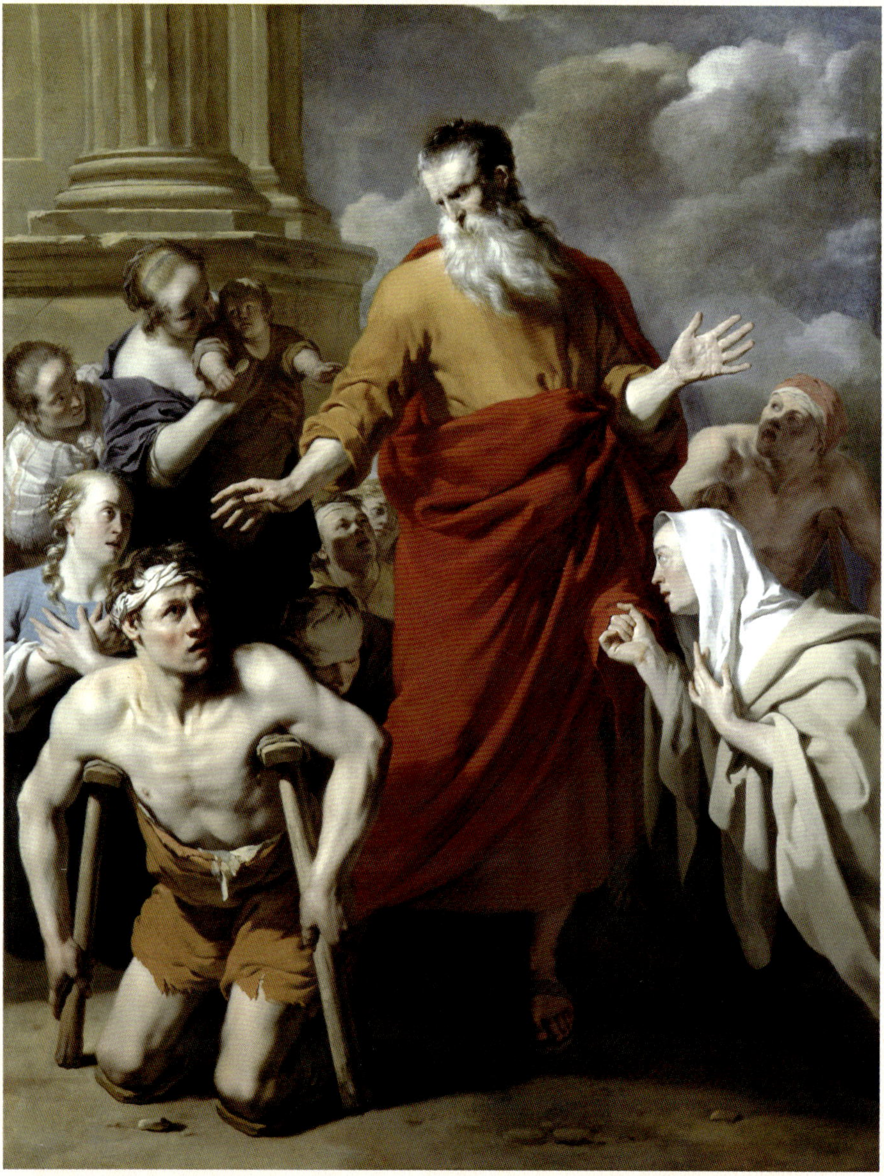

9. ST PAUL HEALING THE CRIPPLE AT LYSTRA
Karel Dujardin

9. St Paul Healing the Cripple at Lystra

Karel Dujardin

Dujardin was a Dutchman who went at least twice to Italy and mainly painted Italianate landscapes with figures. But he also painted the occasional religious subject and, as we can see here, he had a fine sense of atmosphere. St Paul never refers to any miracles, and one would deduce from his writings that he saw them as simply means to a far greater end, that of accepting the Lord Jesus. To know Jesus "and him crucified": for us fallen creatures, that was the supreme miracle. It is St Luke who lovingly details the miracles, and this one is of special importance in that it duplicates a miracle of St Peter's who also healed a cripple, (and this reminds us of how Jesus himself healed cripples and what this gift of physical health was meant to symbolise).

Paul and Barnabas have been driven out from Iconium and are preaching the Gospel in another city, Lystra. "Now at Lystra, there was a man sitting, who could not use his feet; he was a cripple from birth, who had never walked." St Luke who, remember, was a doctor, is anxious that we should understand the full extent of this man's disability, since he tells us in four different ways that he is crippled. Dujardin shows us a strong young man whose shoulder muscles have been over developed by the use of his crutches. He is poor and ragged and, although he is not looking at Paul, we can see that he is listening, with a pathetic eagerness. "He listened to Paul speaking; and Paul looking intently at him and seeing that he had faith to be made well, said in a loud voice, 'stand upright on your feet'. And he sprang up and walked." Dujardin shows us the moment before Paul speaks. He is giving the cripple that unnervingly "intent look" of his, searching into the heart to see how genuine is the man's faith. There seems to be another cripple behind St Paul and there are certainly people praying for help on the right and on the left. But it is only this one man who is cured. Miracles come in response to faith: they are not arbitrary, and there is something in the tension of St Paul's body that suggests that he is almost compelled to this act of healing.

Dujardin's St Paul is a dominating and awe-inspiring figure but he does not conform to the early Christian image. This is a St Paul imagined afresh, without baldness or short black beard.

10.
Paul and Barnabas at Lystra

by Nicolaes Berchem, (1620-1683), 1650,
Musée d'Art, St Etienne, France.

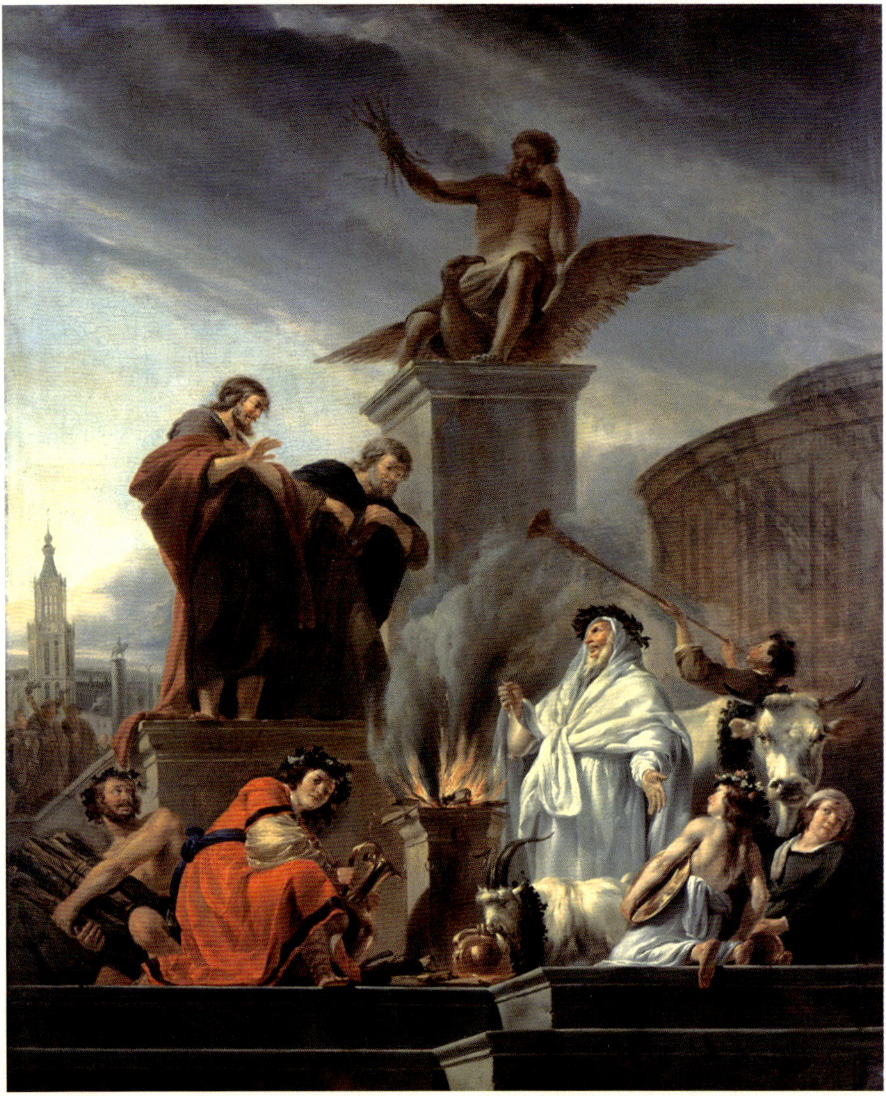

10. PAUL AND BARNABAS AT LYSTRA
Nicolaes Berchem

10. Paul and Barnabas at Lystra

Nicolaes Berchem

Berchem was one of the seventeenth-century Dutch artists, who was enraptured by the golden light of Italy. This is an early painting before he concentrated almost wholly on landscape, but it is so dramatic that one cannot but wish he had painted religious subjects more often.

We see here the startling aftermath of St Paul's miraculous healing of the cripple. Not surprisingly, it made a deep impression on the people of Lystra: the rumour spread that they had received a divine visitation. "When the crowd saw what Paul had done, they lifted up their voices, saying in Lycaonian, 'the gods have come down to us in the likeness of men!' Barnabas, they called Zeus and Paul, because he was the chief speaker, Hermes." There was a charming legend that the gods Zeus and Hermes had once come to earth, seeking hospitality. Nobody welcomed them except the aged husband and wife, Baucis and Philemon. Fairy story that it was, it is nevertheless in line with the teaching of Jesus: "whatsoever you do to the least of my brethren you do unto me." It seems to me very touching that the people of Lystra were determined not to repeat the mistake of their ancestors.

"The priest of Zeus, whose temple was in the front of the city, brought oxen and garlands to the gates and wanted to offer sacrifice with the people." Berchem shows us the priest in ceremonial white, sacrificial ox and goat at the ready, fire lit, trumpet sounding, expectation at the height. It showed a great readiness to believe in God's care for His people but, of course, in a form that horrified the Apostles. "When the Apostles Barnabas and Paul heard of it they tore their garments and rushed out among the multitude, crying, 'men, why are you doing this?

We also are men, of like nature with you…'" Berchem portrays well the astonished horror of the Apostles so unwillingly and paradoxically deified. St Luke concludes sadly, "they scarcely restrained the people from offering sacrifice to them."

Fittingly, this strange episode seems to take place in a misty and dark atmosphere, a great statue of Zeus sitting on his eagle brooding morosely over the misunderstanding. It was a misunderstanding all the more tragic in that Lystra showed an obvious desire and readiness to believe in God, and yet was unable to "turn from these vain things to a living God who made the heaven and earth and the seas and all that is in them."

Despite all the excitement, Paul seems to have had little success in Lystra. The story ends "Jews came there from Antioch and Iconium: and having persuaded the people, they stoned Paul and dragged him out of the city, supposing that he was dead." We cannot help but think of Palm Sunday, when Jesus was made so welcome, and Good Friday when he was cast out and rejected. Paul suffered intensely but mainly because of the terrible loss of these ignorant people. For himself, "he gloried in the cross of Our Lord Jesus Christ."

11.
St Paul Preaching at Athens

by Raphael (1483-1520), c.1513-1514,
Tapestry Cartoon,
Victoria and Albert Museum, London.

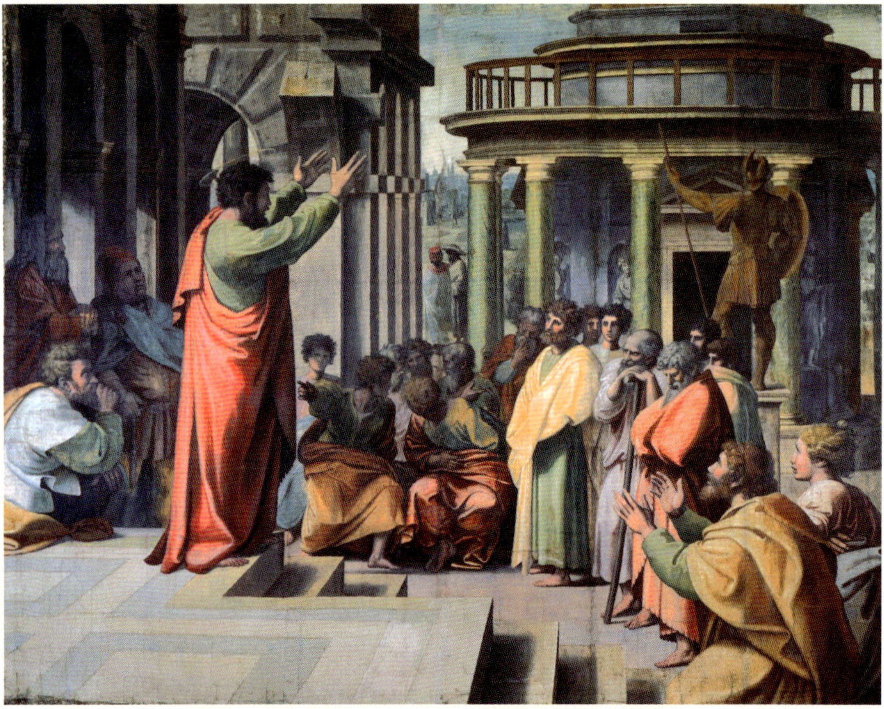

11. ST PAUL PREACHING AT ATHENS
Raphael

11. St Paul Preaching at Athens

Raphael

This is Raphael's second Pauline cartoon, and it is one of his most famous. We in the West consider we draw our civilisation from the Greeks and our religion from the Jews. Raphael, who had a keen appreciation of antiquity, could not resist this unique moment when the great Apostle of the Gentiles stood within the very centre of that civilisation and tried to explain to these professional philosophers, rationalists to the core, the mystery of Jesus. He did not approach them with a great deal of confidence. "His spirit was provoked within him as he saw the city was full of idols. So he argued in the synagogue with the Jews and devout persons, and in the market place every day with those who chanced to be there." It was this "market place" preaching that aroused interest. Athens was home to many philosophers, but St Luke mentions especially the Epicureans and Stoics. "Some said, 'what would this babbler say?' Others, 'he seems to be a preacher of foreign divinities – because he preached Jesus and the resurrection.' And they took hold of him and brought him to the Areopagus."

We then have this touching episode in which Paul puts his whole heart into converting his intellectual congregation. He is courteous and respectful, he quotes "some of your own poets". Whatever Paul hopes, St Luke makes it clear that he cannot expect much of a reception. "All the Athenians and the foreigners who lived there spent their time in nothing except telling or hearing something new." This is unfair, and Raphael does not show us wholesale rejection. The little group immediately to Paul's right may be scoffing with genteel scorn, but the men next to them are clearly puzzled, and the circle continues around to the far right where a man holds up his hands in astonishment. Beside him is one of the most beautiful women that Raphael ever painted: in this setting she can only be a prostitute since no respectable woman would be seen in company with men, hair unbound, listening intently. With their rational disbelief in the after life, the Athenians could not but scoff at the apparent nonsense of a return from death. "Some mocked: but others said, 'we will hear you again about this.'"

The empty courtesy and scorn are both visible in this great painting, with its backdrop of impressive architecture, and the paucity of the congregation. The Athenians were not ready for the overwhelming simplicity of the Gospel. "So Paul went out from among them." St Luke does mention two converts, Dionysius the Areopagite and "a woman named Damarias". I like to think that it is the lovely, wondering face of Damarias that we see here on the right.

12.
St Paul Preaching at Ephesus

by Eustache Le Sueur (1616-1655), 1649,
National Gallery, London.

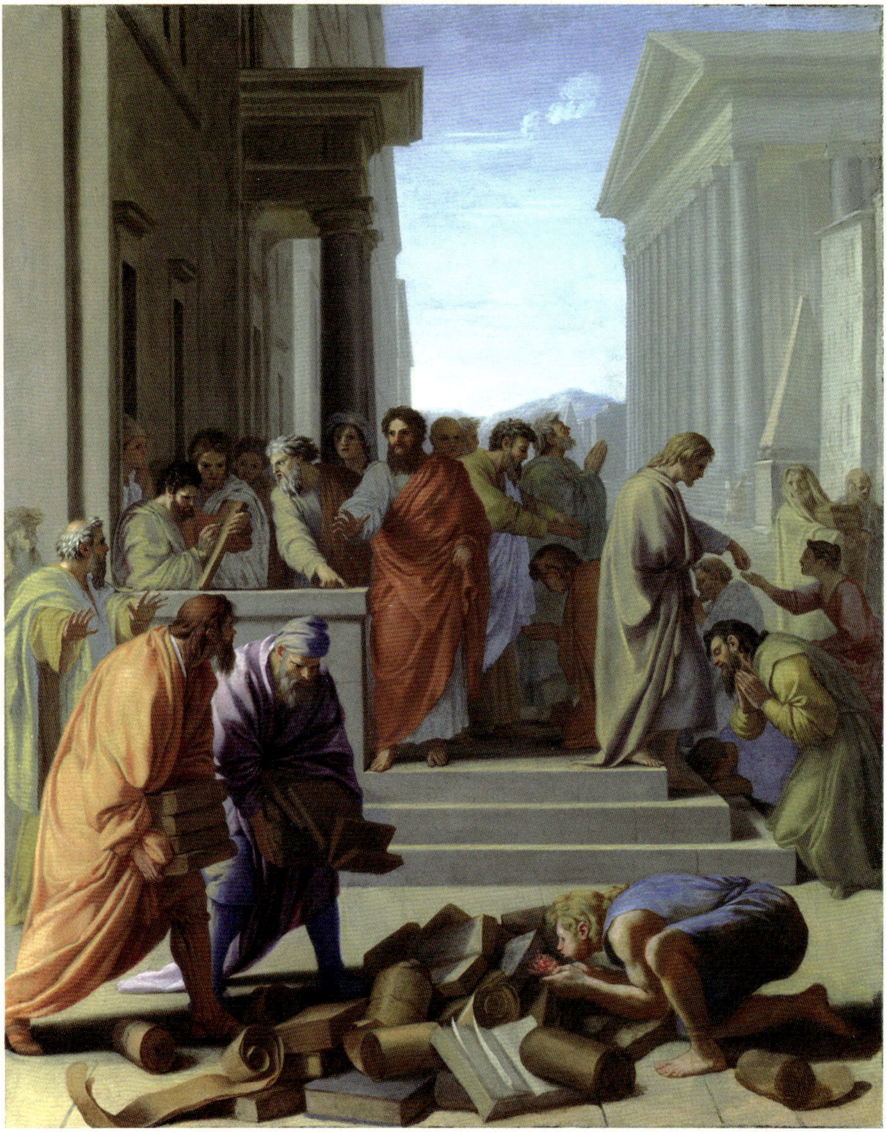

12. ST PAUL PREACHING AT EPHESUS
Eustache Le Sueur

12. St Paul Preaching at Ephesus

Eustache Le Sueur

Le Sueur, at his best, has a touch of the majesty of Poussin. Here he depicts one of the many events that happened when St Paul was in Ephesus. He stayed in that great city for two years and, says St Luke, "God did extraordinary miracles by the hand of Paul, so that handkerchiefs or aprons were carried away from his body to the sick and diseases left them and the evil spirits came out of them." It was these "evil spirits" that caused the trouble for St Paul. Ephesus was a deeply superstitious city, notorious for the freedom of its sexual behaviour and for the importance of their great goddess: Diana of the Ephesians. St Paul drove out evil spirits but had nothing but contempt for the magical practices that were so prevalent in Ephesus and from which so many inhabitants drew their income. His power, which was solely that of the Gospel, terrified the pagans and drew many to come humbly to the Apostles' feet to hear the Gospels. But among these "who were now believers" there were magicians or soothsayers or exorcists. These men who had now been blessed by the clarity of the Gospel, confessed to Paul the dark ways in which they had previously earned their living. "And a number of those who practiced magic arts brought their books together and burned them in the sight of all; and they counted the value of them and found it came to 50,000 pieces of silver."

It is this great burning that Le Sueur shows us. The picture is divided into two. In the foreground are the new converts heaping up their magical books and their scrolls. The fire is already being kindled. There is a sense here of haste and even anger: perhaps they resent the deceptions in which they had been unconsciously ensnared. Behind them, separated by a flight of steps, the Apostles are concerned with the word of God. Le Sueur, seventeenth-century sophisticate, uses no halo to set Paul apart, but he is surely the dark man in a blue tunic and a red cloak urging on the destruction of dangerous literature. Around him the central activities of a Christian church continue. On the right, one of the Apostles gives alms to the poor, in the centre there are prayers of blessing and on the left a scribe (perhaps St Luke?) seems to be jotting down St Paul's words. I hope he is not merely adding up the value of the burnt books, which obviously made a great impression on all who saw it.

This is a strange picture, again with a rather atypical St Paul, but it does bring home to us the violent side-effects that, of necessity, accompany the peaceful preaching of the Gospel. There is a certain homelessness about Le Sueur's St Paul. The great classic buildings soar up on either side, squeezing him out, shutting him into a narrow space, in which alone he is free to follow the example of Jesus, loving, giving, blessing, preaching, healing.

13.
St Paul on Malta

by Adam Elsheimer (1578-1610), c.1600,
National Gallery, London.

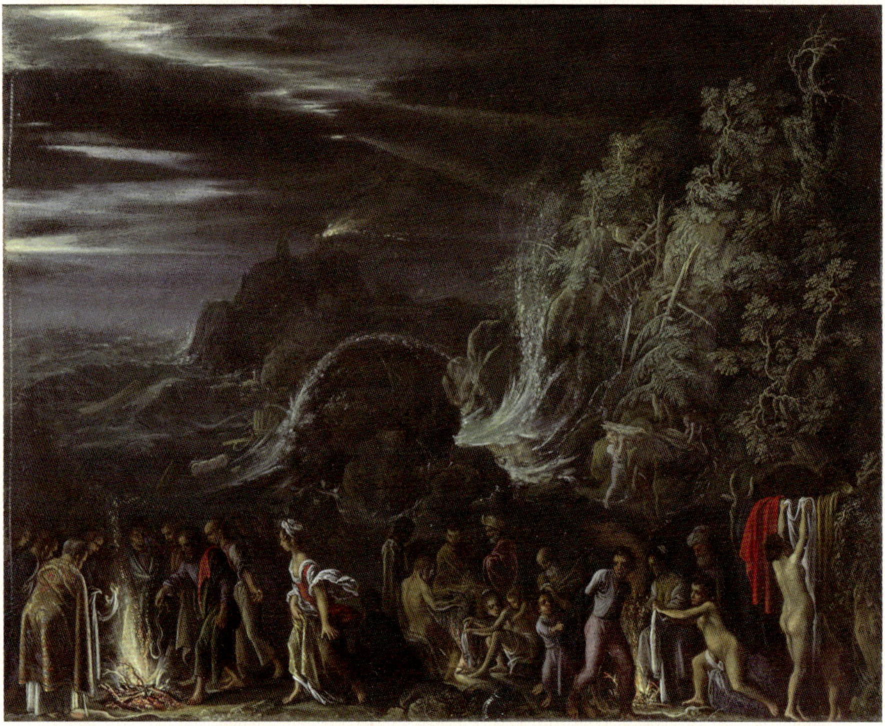

13. ST PAUL ON MALTA
Adam Elsheimer

13. St Paul on Malta

Adam Elsheimer

Saint Paul tells us that he was shipwrecked three times, adding for greater emphasis, "a night and a day I have been adrift at sea". St Luke, highly skilled as an editor and storyteller, only gives us one account of a shipwreck, all the more dramatic for that, and all the more powerful in its position in the story. He tells us, in considerable detail, of the journey to Italy as a prisoner bound for Rome. It is a wonderfully dramatic story, and shows Paul at his human best: wise, practical, unperturbed by disaster. (His only failing, very understandable, when his advice has been ignored, is to say "you should have listened to me.") Mainly due to Paul's advice, his guards, the crew and all the prisoners arrive safely on Malta. But their safe arrival was achieved against all odds, and Elsheimer gives us a portrait of a shipwreck par-excellence.

It is night, the moon gleams through the dark obscurity of the sky, catching on the cascades of wild waves and casting an eerie glimmer on the broken foliage of the coast. St Luke adds "it had begun to rain and it was cold". The inhabitants, who welcomed those rescued from the shipwreck (with unusual kindness) made a fire, which Elsheimer shows as the other source of light in his night-time drama. There is the cold light of the moon above and the warmer glow of the fires below. Unembarrassed passengers (notice the lovely lady at the far right and her semi-naked companions in the centre) are drying their clothes. The Apostle and his guards huddle fully clothed, as one might expect, around the larger fire on the left. There were to be dramatic happenings at Malta, but Elsheimer concentrates on the frightening reality of a storm at sea, with a perilous swim to dry land.

If we think of this, not as unique in Paul's life, but as a fearsome hardship he endured several times, we can understand why he can "boast" of the grace of God that made it possible for him to endure so many dangers and hardships "through many a sleepless night, in hunger and thirst, often without food, in cold and exposure". In giving his life to the Gospel, he accepted that he would know all the fears and physical uncertainties of a marginal life. In this, he felt he imitated Jesus. "For he was crucified in weakness, but lives by the power of God. For we are weak in Him, but… we shall live with him by the power of God." "We are glad when we are weak."

14.
St Paul with the Viper

Wall painting in Canterbury Cathedral.

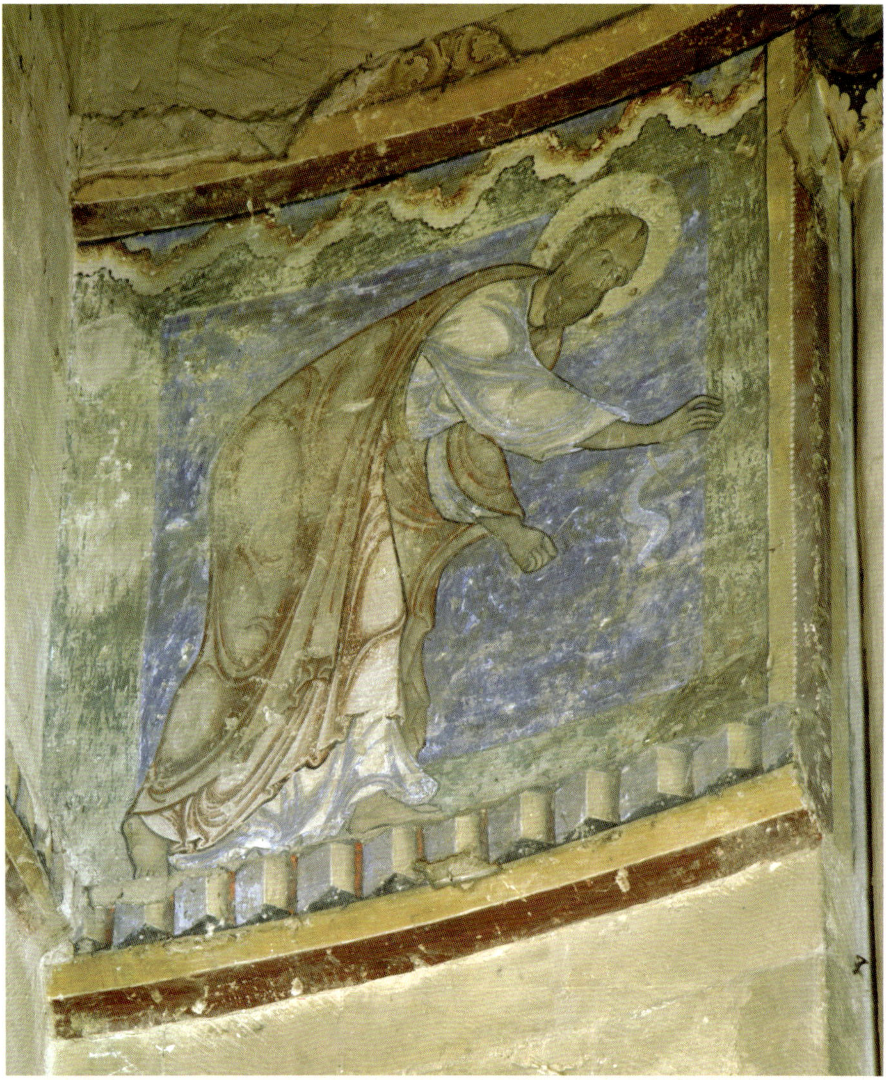

14. ST PAUL WITH THE VIPER
Wall painting in Canterbury Cathedral

14. St Paul with the Viper

Wall painting in Canterbury Cathedral

Henry VIII devastated the English churches in his quest for their treasures. What he left undone was savagely completed by Cromwell, very little interested in treasure, but deeply concerned with the "idolatry" of religious images. Hardly any of the wall paintings that glorified God and taught our ancestors their faith have survived. But this great painting of St Paul can still be seen in Canterbury Cathedral. It is not all that easy to see, you have to askew your neck, and the paint is faint, but it is a precious relic of the age of faith.

However, we need to know the story to make sense of it. The unknown artist, who seems to me to be a major artist, with a lovely amplitude of form, is telling the story of St Paul after his shipwreck at Malta. "Paul had gathered a bundle of sticks and put them on the fire," (generously kindled for them by the kindly Maltese), "when a viper came out because of the heat and fastened on his hand." When the natives saw the creature hanging from his hand, they said to one another, "no doubt this man is a murderer. Though he has escaped from the sea, justice has not allowed him to live. He, however, shook off the creature into the fire and suffered no harm." One can imagine the excitement: they could see for themselves how God's justice was not mocked, and this well-spoken villain had received the reward for his crimes. St Luke enjoys the irony. "They waited, expecting him to swell up or suddenly fall down dead; but when they had waited a long time, (surely St Luke is smiling?) and saw no misfortune come to him, they changed their minds and said he was a god." This was not the first time St Paul's spiritual power made the superstitious consider him a god, but the Canterbury artist is not concerned with anybody's reaction except St Paul's. He has bent down to put sticks on the fire, he has been bitten "the viper has fastened on his hand" and here he is shaking it off into the fire, with unruffled aplomb.

What the artist wants to show us is the certainty of Divine protection. St Paul knows that he has been chosen for a great work and that, whatever he suffers, whatever the obstacles, his Lord will preserve him. He may not have preserved him from the actual pain of the bite (for the Christian, suffering should be redemptive), but he preserves him from its ill-effects. In a few minutes he will stand upright, ignoring the pain, and continue steadily the work of God.

15.
Miracles of St Paul

Right half of an ivory diptych,
early fifth century
Bargello, Florence, Italy.

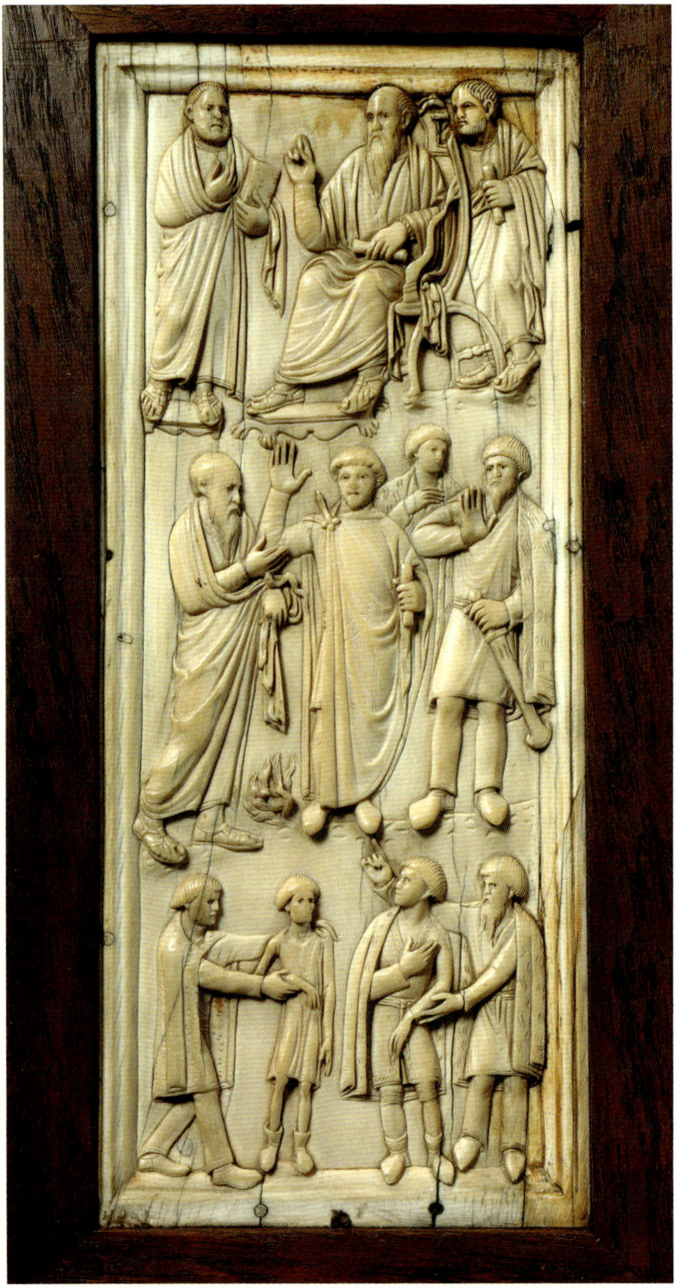

15. MIRACLES OF ST PAUL
Right half of an ivory diptych

15. Miracles of St Paul

Right half of an ivory diptych

On ceremonial occasions, Roman high officials distributed to fellow aristocrats ivory panels, usually made in two parts, (that is a diptych). On the whole, the early church was poor, with few nobles or dignitaries in its congregations. But by the fifth century, there was the occasional believer who could commission a diptych of real quality. The left leaf of this work of art shows a magnificent Adam naming the animals in Eden. The right leaf, shown here, depicts St Paul as in control of the animal world, as was Adam in Eden.

The message is conveyed on three levels. At the top we see St Paul seated in the chair of authority explaining the word of the Lord. It may be that St Luke stands before him holding the book in which he will write about St Paul's preaching, and another Apostle, (Barnabas? Mark?) stands behind him to emphasise that St Paul speaks from the heart of the Church.

The second scene shows the encounter with the viper that happened at Malta. The well-dressed gentleman, next to St Paul, is almost certainly "the chief man of the island, named Publius", while behind him are the astonished commoners waiting for St Paul to fall dead. Scholars point out that Publius wears Roman garb and the other two seem to be German bodyguards. St Paul appears to wince a little as the viper bites home, but he is calm and in control. St Luke tells us that St Paul healed the father of Publius who was "sick with fever and dysentery" and after this "the rest of the people on the island who had diseases also came and were cured".

The bottom line shows the Maltese sick, the emaciated boy, the man who seems to have heart disease, and their friends who bring them into the presence of the Apostle. The point is not easy to grasp but it seems to me that we are shown that it is God who is in control of our physical life. Paul, so serenely aware of the presence of Jesus, communicates by every word and gesture, by the faith that consumes him, the power to rise above physical weakness. Jesus is our health in the most profound sense, and to receive his love, his redemption, is to be set free "whether for life or for death".

16.
St Paul in Prison

by Rembrandt (1606-1669), 1627,
Staatsgalerie, Stuttgart, Germany.

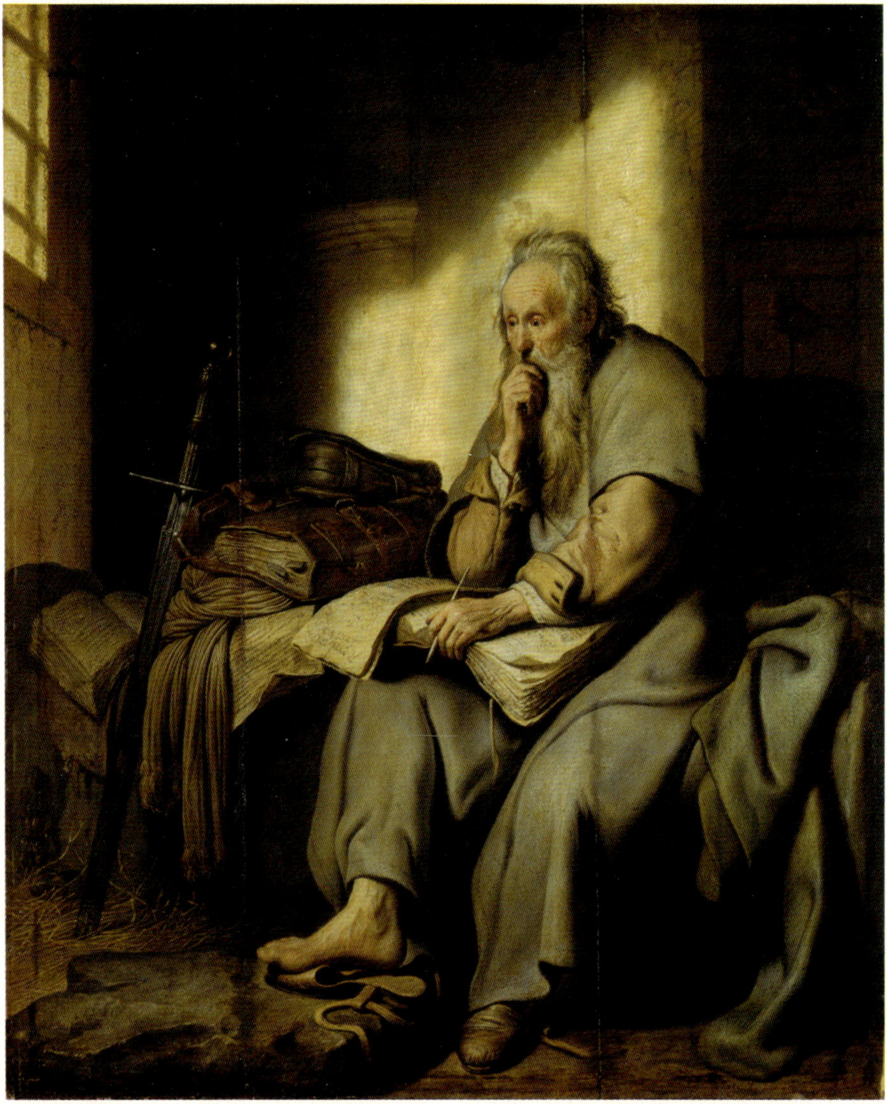

16. ST PAUL IN PRISON
Rembrandt

16. St Paul in Prison

Rembrandt

When St Paul appealed "to Caesar" it meant that he travelled under guard to Rome and, until his appeal was heard, was technically in prison. Modern scholarship tells us that it was not imprisonment in the strict sense but more what we would call "house arrest". Yet even this was a severe curtailment of Paul's missionary longings: for all his courage, it must have been a long period of intense frustration. It is these interior sufferings, the emotions of the heart, that Rembrandt so uniquely understands.

He portrays an elderly Paul, all that black hair blanched to white, slumped disconsolately in his prison cell – "prison cell, or room under house arrest" either description applies. He seems to have no chair and to be sitting on his bed. His feet that have trudged over so much of the near East, now slip wearily out of their sandals. He has nowhere to go. Tantalisingly, a radiance gleams upon the saint and his imprisoning wall through the window, reminding him of the outside world into which he may not travel. Rembrandt sees St Paul as striving to make his imprisonment fruitful, to use it for the good of the Church, as he has used all that has happened to him. "Now I rejoice in my sufferings for your sake, and in my flesh I complete what is lacking in Christ's afflictions for the sake of His Body, that is the Church… though I am absent in body, yet I am with you in Spirit."

St Paul is praying and thinking, holding in one hand the pen with which he will write to his disciples. His world has become completely interior and yet it contains all that is dear to the heart of God, the needs of those who do not know Him and those that do. Perhaps by setting St Paul between a patch of luminous brightness and a great rectangle of darkness, Rembrandt is suggesting that the saint is poised between life and death. After his two years of house arrest, he was arrested again and executed.

As often happens in Rembrandt's work, there is a grave dignity that makes us aware of the seriousness of mortal life. St Paul tells us that he was not by nature an orator. He speaks of himself as "unskilled in speaking", but not "in knowledge". He knew that God had enlightened him and that it was his responsibility to share with the church everything that God had given him: he was after all an "Apostle", a messenger. Yet, as one who struggled to speak effectively, it must have been a heavy burden to find the words that revealed Christ Jesus. Rembrandt, most empathic of artists, imagines Paul wrestling with language so that he could bless his converts with the riches that come from the grace of God.

17.
St Paul Sends the Letter to the Ephesians

Miniature from an illuminated manuscript,
thirteenth century,
Biblioteca Marciana, Venice.

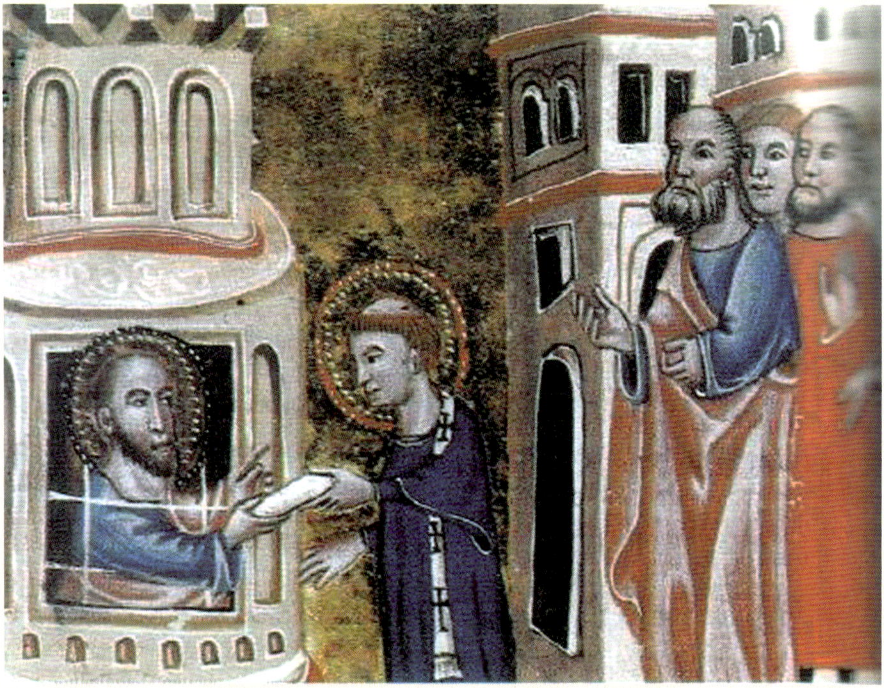

17. ST PAUL SENDS THE LETTER TO THE EPHESIANS
Miniature from an illuminated manuscript

17. St Paul Sends the Letter to the Ephesians

Miniature from an illuminated manuscript

This delightful miniature imagines a rather youthful looking Paul thrusting his arms through the bars of his prison as he hands over the letter he has just written to the Ephesians. To whom is he handing it? Who is the affable young cleric with a halo, reverently receiving the precious epistle? The Letter to the Ephesians says at the end: "Now that you also may know how I am and what I am doing, Tychicus, the beloved brother and faithful minister in the Lord, will tell you everything. I have sent him to you for this very purpose, that you may know how we are, and that he may encourage your hearts." The Letter to the Ephesians is very much a letter aware of imprisonment. Paul asks for prayers "that utterance may be given me in opening my mouth boldly to proclaim the mystery of the Gospel, for which I am an ambassador in chains."

Modern scholarship is not wholly certain that Ephesians is a personal letter written by St Paul, but they agree that it is written in his name and expresses his teaching. More than once he speaks of his status as "a prisoner of Christ Jesus on behalf of you gentiles" and his eagerness "to preach to the gentiles the unsearchable riches of Christ, and to make all men see what is the plan of the mystery hidden for ages in God."

The unknown artist who painted this little miniature expresses beautifully the affection between the saint and his messenger, whether Tychicus or some other "beloved brother", and also the longing of the Ephesians to receive his letter. There they stand on the right with the great buildings of Ephesus as their background, waiting eagerly to receive through the Church, "the manifold wisdom of God". St Paul asks them "not to lose heart for what I am suffering for you, which is your glory." It is quite obvious from this little picture that the Ephesians have not "lost heart" and are only too ready to hear what the letter will tell them. The saint seems to have a soft spot for the Ephesians, calling them, "beloved children" and the way that they stretch out their hands suggests that they have an equal affection for him.

It is difficult for us, so many centuries later, to realise how unsettling it must have been for the early Christians when the missionary journeys stopped and Paul, that great wanderer for Christ, was shut up in one place and that they would never again see him. Receiving his letters must have been a source of enormous encouragement, and the air of happy complicity, as if the letter was being smuggled out, shows that St Paul is aware of the significance of this correspondence. The miniature comes from a manuscript that contains this particular letter but, in fact, it could have been any of his letters from prison, all vital to their respective churches.

18.
St Paul

by Aidan Hart, contemporary,
from St John's Bible, Collegeville, U.S.A.

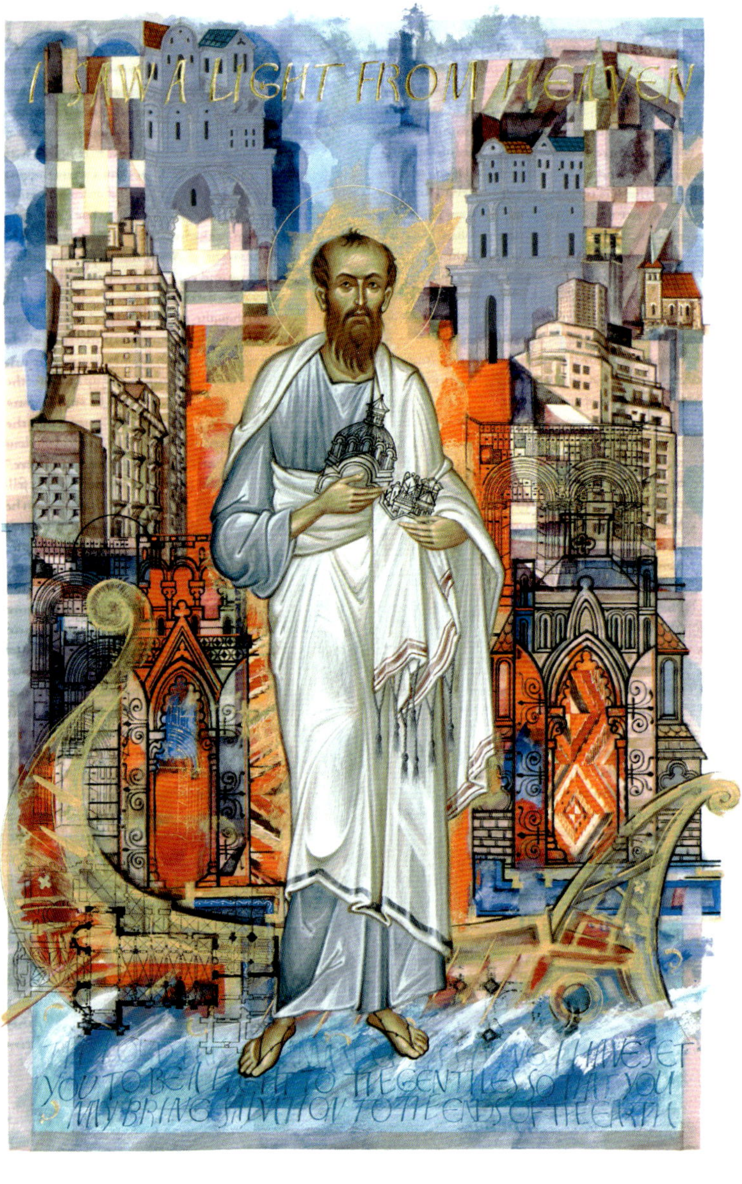

18. ST PAUL
Aidan Hart

18. St Paul

Aidan Hart

The Benedictine monks of St John's Abbey in Minnesota gave the church and the world a gift of unique magnificence in honour of the millennium. They commissioned a hand written illuminated bible and asked Donald Jackson to direct the team that would produce it. Much of the exquisite calligraphy and the illuminations are by Jackson himself but he asked Aidan Hart, the well-known iconographer, to paint this picture of St Paul for the Acts of the Apostles.

Hart understands that St Paul is profoundly a Jew and shows him wearing a Jewish prayer shawl. He also shows him against a rich kaleidoscope of churches, old and new. The welfare of these churches, when he was no longer at hand to guide them, must have been a source of deep anxiety to Paul in prison. When he sums up what he has suffered for the sake of the Gospel, his climax is "the daily pressure upon me of my anxiety for all the churches". He explains why: "Who is weak and I am not weak? Who is made to fall, and I am not indignant?" It was not so much, he thought, the churches needed him in his weak capacity, but that his very weakness enabled him to understand their need to turn to God. So, ironically, I see this tall, elegant Paul as Paul at the end of his journeyings, in prison. Behind him is a Roman ship: he will travel no more. And still further behind, are images of all the churches that will be built in the centuries after his death.

He himself of course, never knew what we think of as a "church". His converts met in one another's houses, and it was not for several centuries that the Christians dared to erect actual buildings. But, because of Paul, there will be Gothic churches and Romanesque churches, there will be Renaissance churches and Contemporary churches. At his left elbow are arches from the entrance to the Basilica of the Holy Sepulchre in Jerusalem. Above that, near the margin, is the little Chapel of Stella Maris that stands in the grounds of St John's Abbey and next to that the sublime, modernistic cross of the Abbey cemetery. St Paul was a city man, and so Hart surrounds him with the high rise buildings that dominate contemporary cities. Most poignantly he holds in his hands and to his heart what looks like St Peter's Basilica in Rome, but split in two. It could be that Hart is calling to mind the use the early reformers made of St Paul's writings, and this may explain his look of gentle sadness. Paul longed for the unity of the Church. That he would be used to divide it would have been a heartbreak for him.

19.
Sarcophagus of Junius Bassus

Detail c.359 AD,
Treasury of St Peters, Vatican City.

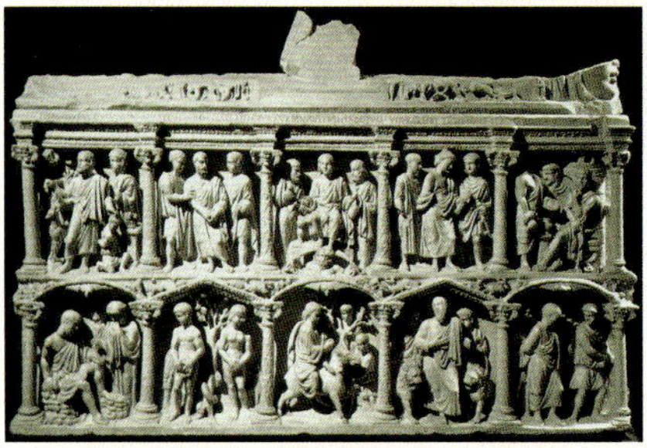

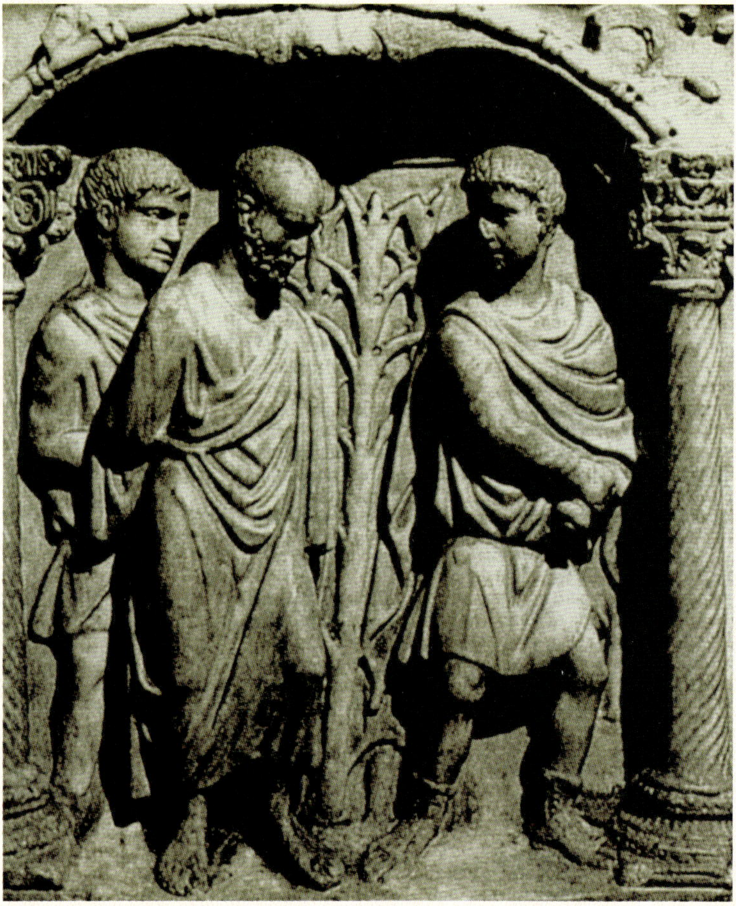

19. SARCOPHAGUS OF JUNIUS BASSUS, DETAIL

19. Sarcophagus of Junius Bassus, detail

Wealthy Romans were buried in sarcophagi, poor Christians in a niche in the catacombs. But by the fourth century there was an occasional Christian, very occasional, who was also a wealthy Roman, and such a one was Junius Bassus. He was the Prefect of Rome, an important position, and he must have been following the faith for some time before he fell sick and was baptised on his deathbed. His marble sarcophagus is of great beauty, and contains images both of the Old Testament and the New, all recalling redemption and the power of God.

Among these images is this powerful carving of St Paul being led to his death. He is bound, "an Apostle in chains", and seems to be intent on living what he has preached. "Be strong in the Lord and in the strength of his might... that you may be able to withstand in the evil day, and having done all, to stand. Stand therefore, having girded your loins with truth." This is a man completely at peace. "For me to live is Christ, and to die is gain." The soldiers who lead him to death seem to be influenced by his air of serious tranquillity. St Paul knew that Jesus said on the cross "Father forgive them for they know not what they do." He had actually heard St Stephen fall dying to the ground saying "Lord, hold not this sin to their charge." We can be certain that in the years in which St Paul awaited his execution, he would have schooled himself to go to death with the same prayer upon his lips.

As the rich and important Junius Bassus contemplated his own death, this was the sort of example that he felt helpful. It emphasised that for a Christian death was not all that important. "Christ loved us and gave himself up for us, a fragrant offering and sacrifice to God." St Paul, head bowed in prayer, is walking towards his physical participation in that sacrifice. Perhaps significantly, as a symbol, the sculptor has set beside St Paul what looks like a many-branched tree. Because Paul accepted his weakness, and allowed God to be his strength, the faith he planted during his journeys was to branch out to the ends of the earth. He must have felt an immense gratitude to the God who had achieved so much through him. He could never stress enough "the immeasurable greatness of His power in us who believe." It was never, for Paul, his own power; only and always the power of Jesus.

20.
The Beheading of St Paul

by Alessandro Algardi (1595-1654), 1650,
San Paulo Maggiore, Bologna, Italy.

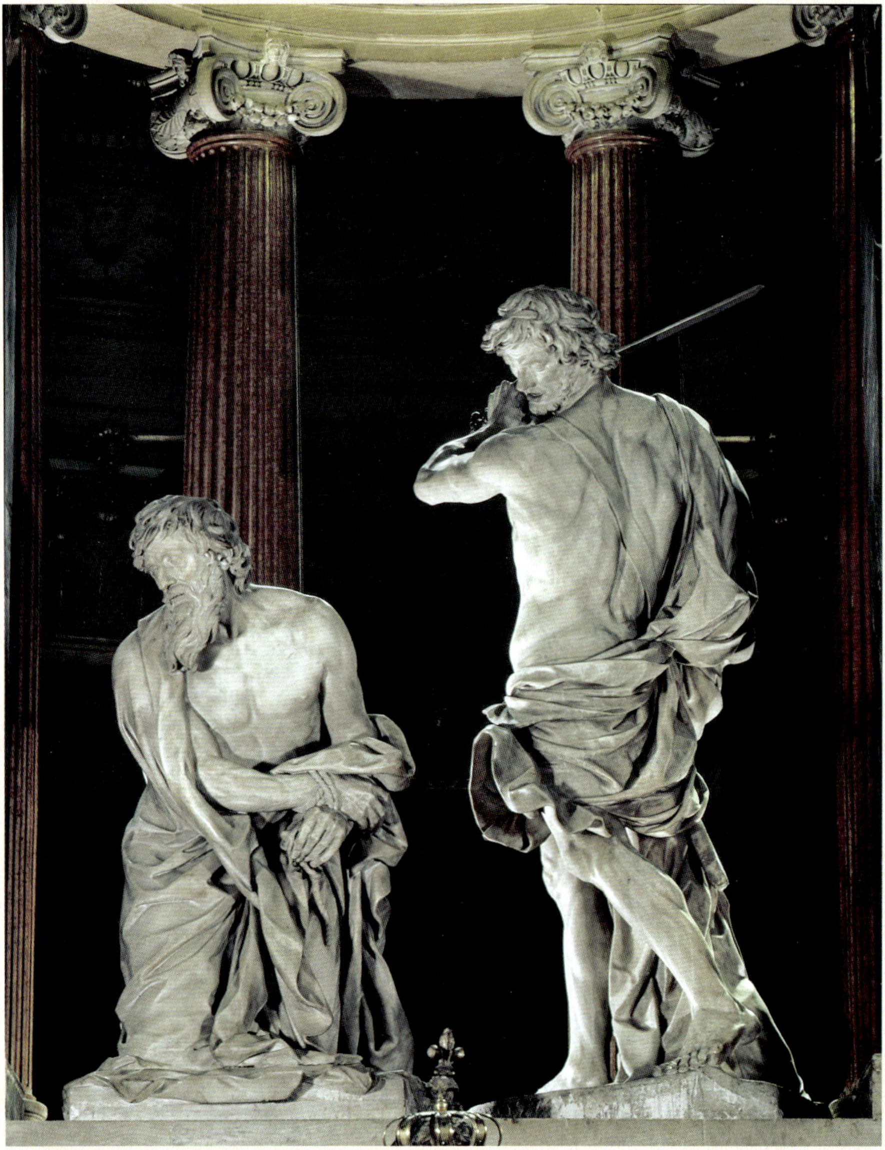

20. THE BEHEADING OF ST PAUL
Alessandro Algardi

20. The Beheading of St Paul

Alessandro Algardi

For most of his life, Algardi was overshadowed by the great Bernini, whose dramatic sculptures were so appreciated in Rome. Algardi was far more restrained, more classical, and only towards the end of his life, when Bernini had a period of disgrace, (there were many ups and downs in the political excitements of Rome) did he receive his rightful recognition.

This great work, for St Paul's own church in Bologna, shows all the dignified power of which Algardi was capable. St Paul, on his knees, hands bound, still a man at the height of his powers, awaits the executioner's stroke. He averts his head, and seems to be completely at peace. His executioner, a youth of majestic muscularity, raises his sword to strike with immense force. Even the executioner, so graceful in movement, looks at the saint with what one could read as compassion. Algardi does not set up the two forms in opposition. Here is not "good" and "bad" but rather, two men doing their duty. One is executing a man whom he must believe is an enemy of the State: the other is surrendering peacefully to the situation in which he finds himself. For Paul, who so profoundly understood the meaning of the resurrection, "those who have fallen asleep in Christ" have not "perished". When Jesus rose from the dead, he was "the first fruits of those who had fallen asleep… for as in Adam all die, so also in Christ shall all remain alive." We shall pass through death, it has no hold on us. Paul put it with almost lyric power: "for this perishable nature must put on the imperishable, and this mortal nature must put on immortality. When the perishable puts on the imperishable, and the mortal puts on immortality, then shall come to pass the saying that is written: "death is swallowed up in victory" (St Paul is quoting Isaiah). Then he goes on to quote Hosea, "Oh death, where is thy victory? Oh death, where is thy sting?" He ends this great affirmation of his faith in the redemptive power of the cross: "Thanks be to God, who gives us the victory through Our Lord Jesus Christ."

Algardi is not showing us a man defeated, but a man who was soberly and trustingly aware of the victory of Jesus. He may grieve to be leaving unprotected the small congregations of Christians whom he had brought into the light of God wherever he had travelled. Yet, St Paul never saw himself as over-important: he was only an instrument. Those submissive hands and the peaceful droop of his head make it clear that he surrenders this instrument to Him who called him into being.

21.
The Ecstasy of St Paul

Nicolas Poussin (1594-1665), 1649-50,
Louvre, Paris, France.

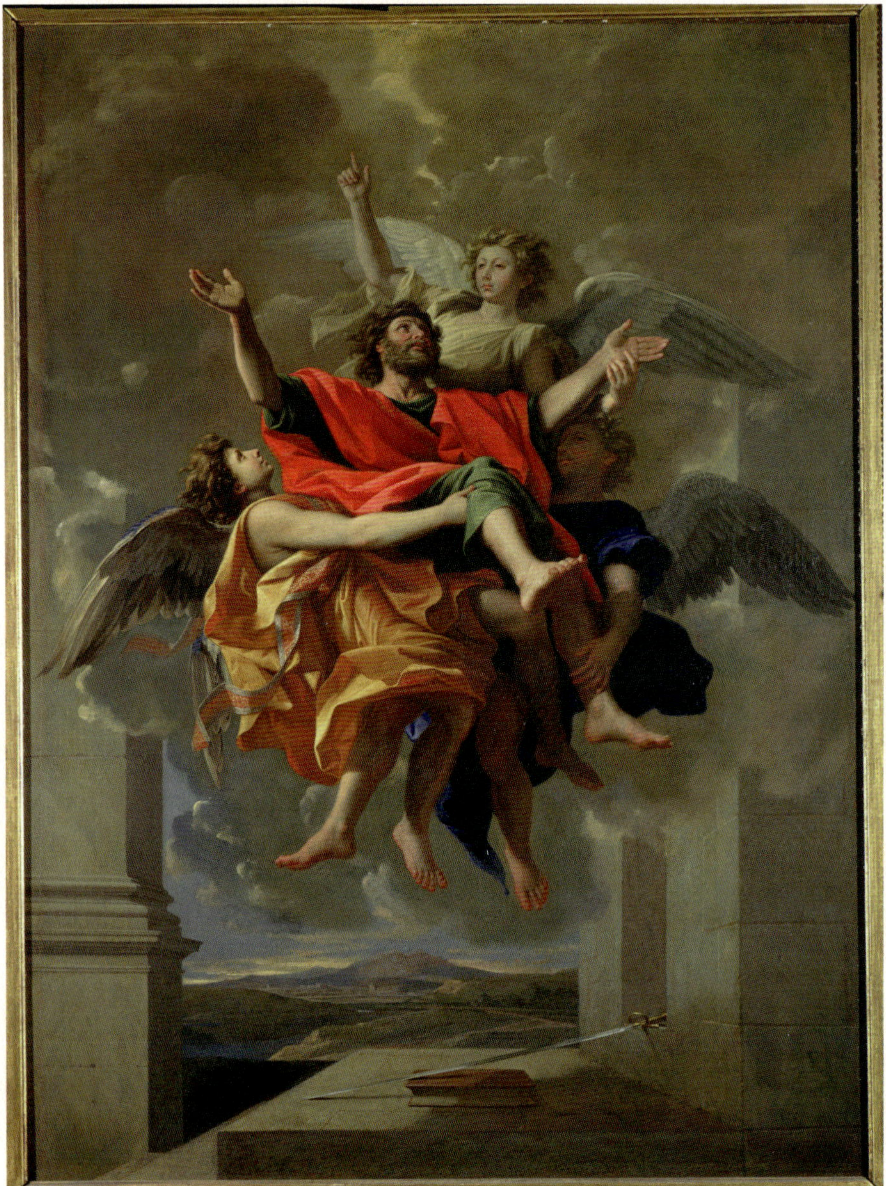

21. THE ECSTASY OF ST PAUL
Nicolas Poussin

21. The Ecstasy of St Paul

Nicolas Poussin

Only Poussin, that most serious and profound of artists, (only Cezanne excels him) could have dared to depict such a topic. It would seem that we are seeing St Paul after his execution carried up to the heavens in which he most ardently believed. In a sense, this is true, St Paul did pass from death to the wonder of eternal life. "For me to live is Christ, and to die is gain." "It has not entered into the heart of man to conceive what God has prepared for those who love Him." But, in fact, Poussin is not depicting the martyred St Paul being lifted by angels to the heavens, but the living St Paul, drawn up from the earth by the passion of his prayer.

Few of us would like to talk about our prayer. It is something intensely personal, that sacred arena in which our weakness surrenders to the greatness of God, and we are lifted out of our smallness, our pettiness, into His infinite freedom. Yet no work has ever been done for God that was not inspired by and supported by and made possible by the grace of God that is given to us in prayer. Of ourselves we can do nothing: it is all gift, all God's doing "God has sent the Spirit of His Son into our hearts, crying, 'Abba! Father!'" Our very prayer is not "our" prayer but it is the Spirit of Jesus praising and loving the Father.

Perhaps no missionary has ever laboured and suffered more for the Gospel than St Paul. It follows, then, that no missionary has ever prayed with the selfless intensity of St Paul. When he is speaking about what he has endured for the sake of the Gospel, he humbly confesses that he is "boasting" but that is at the end of the long list of what he has suffered. Yet, he feels he must add "there is nothing to be gained by it, but I will go on to the visions and revelations of the Lord. I know a man in Christ who fourteen years ago was caught up into the third heaven – whether in the body or out of the body I do not know, God knows. And I know that this man was caught up into Paradise – whether in the body or out of the body I do not know, God knows – and he heard things that cannot be told, which man may not utter. On behalf of this man I will boast but on my own behalf I will not boast, except of my weaknesses." This is one of the most moving passages in St Paul. Ecstasy refers to a state in which one is outside the ego, drawn up into something far greater. It cannot have been a common occurrence in St Paul's life, because he dates it precisely fourteen years ago. What this passage makes quite clear though, in the humblest of ways, is that St Paul had indeed been "caught up". He had known that ecstatic union in which Jesus and one's own spirit seem indistinguishable "to me, to live is Christ".

Various artists have attempted to show various saints in this overwhelming experience of God, and mostly they have little in their painterly repertoire but upturned eyes and a look of amazement. Poussin goes the whole way. His Paul is literally one "caught up", raised above the solidities of the world in which he labours and utterly surrendered, intelligently and in full command of his will, to the God who is the sole significance of his existence. "The life I now live in the flesh, I live by faith in the Son of God, who loved me and who gave Himself for me." "I have been crucified with Christ; it is no longer I who live, but Christ who lives in me." It is not so difficult to say these things, but Paul lives them. Poussin shows him leaving behind on the hard stone of the world, his two attributes: the sword and the book. They represent St Paul, that is how we know him artistically. But this St Paul, has no attributes and no self of his own. He is totally drawn into the wonder of God.

22.
St Paul Enthroned

by Domenico Beccafumi (1484-1551), c.1515,
Museo dell'Opera, Del Duoma, Siena, Italy.

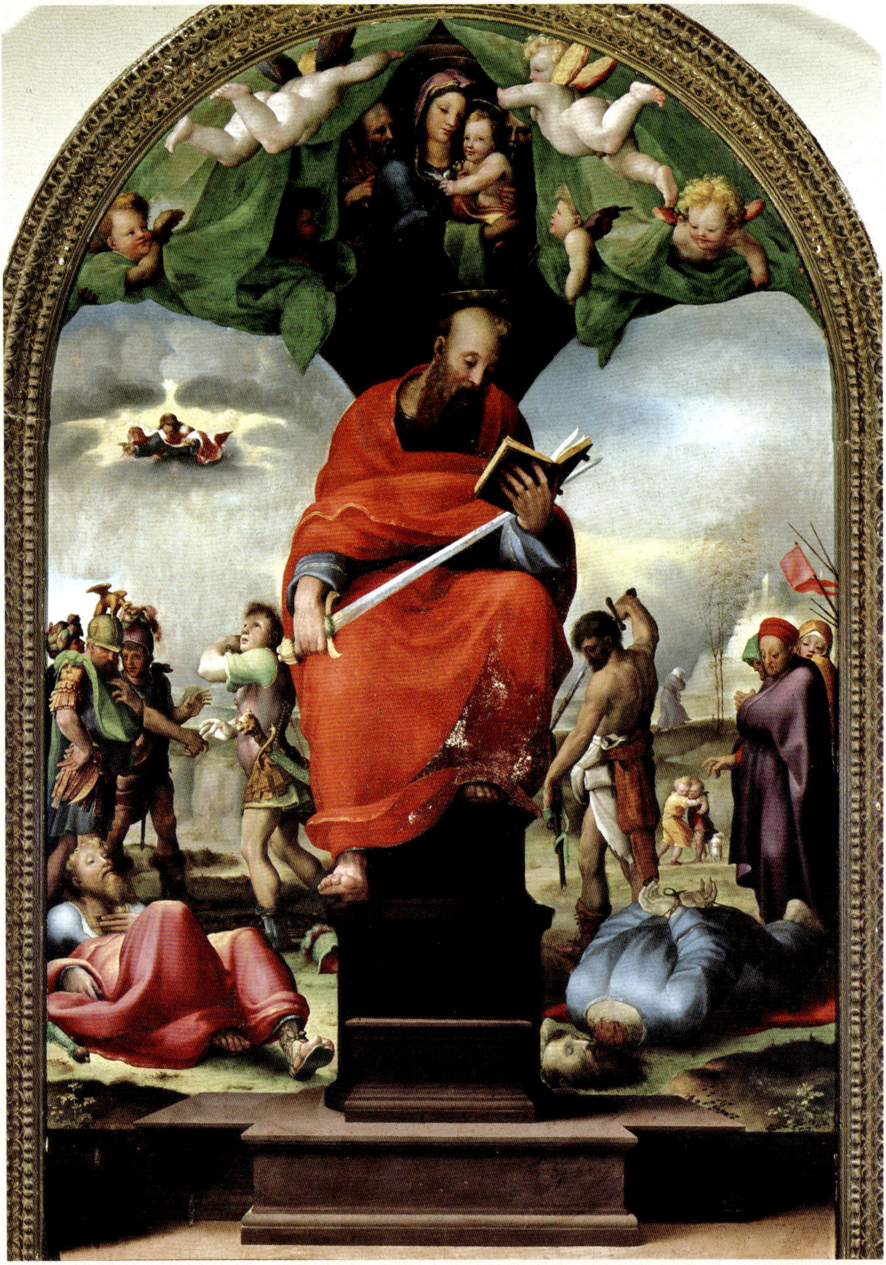

22. ST PAUL ENTHRONED
Domenico Beccafumi

22. St Paul Enthroned

Domenico Beccafumi

From Duccio, in the mid thirteenth century, the city of Siena was blessed by a succession of great artists. Their glory ended in the mid sixteenth century with Beccafumi, last of the great Sienese, and one of the most interesting. He deploys an extraordinary subtlety of colour, acid and arresting, and an unrivalled personal intensity.

This great altarpiece is a compendium of the life of St Paul. He is enthroned, rather uncomfortably, on a severe plinth which widens out above his head to encompass Mary and the infant Jesus, surrounded by playful cherubs. Playful cherubs are not exactly in Paul's line, he is a saint of sublime concentration, but in this apotheosis he sits partially at ease, one foot secure, one foot dangling while he reads the word of God and holds loosely in his lap the sword of his martyrdom.

On either side Beccafumi shows us the two crucial events of Paul's life. On the left, he has been struck to earth, blinded by the light of God. The living Jesus speaks to him from the clouds, while the soldiers, with whom he travels on his mission of persecution, look wonderingly down on their humiliated companion. The fallen Paul on the left is balanced by the fallen Paul on the right, but this is a Paul laid low by death. The executioner sheathes his sword and his disciples look on with grief. The first Paul, Paul on the way to Damascus, has only the company of perplexed fellow travellers. The second Paul, martyred in Rome, has loving disciples and an active enemy in the State. Between the executioner and the mourners, neatly cradled by the bound hands of the dead Paul, are two small children, reminiscent of the infant Jesus and the infant St John. Beccafumi makes no pretence that these scenes are realistic. He is recalling to mind the great trajectory of Paul's journey from that youthful vision on the way to Damascus to that martyr's death outside Rome. He is now above it all. "He has run the race, he has finished the course." He is now at rest in joy. "Now I know in part [he is speaking of his earthly life] then I shall understand fully even as I have been fully understood." This is a St Paul remote from all his travails and agonies, understanding as he is "fully understood".

Saint Paul in Art

Part Two

23.
St Paul

Unknown mosaic artist, fifth century,
Arian Baptistry Ravenna, Italy.

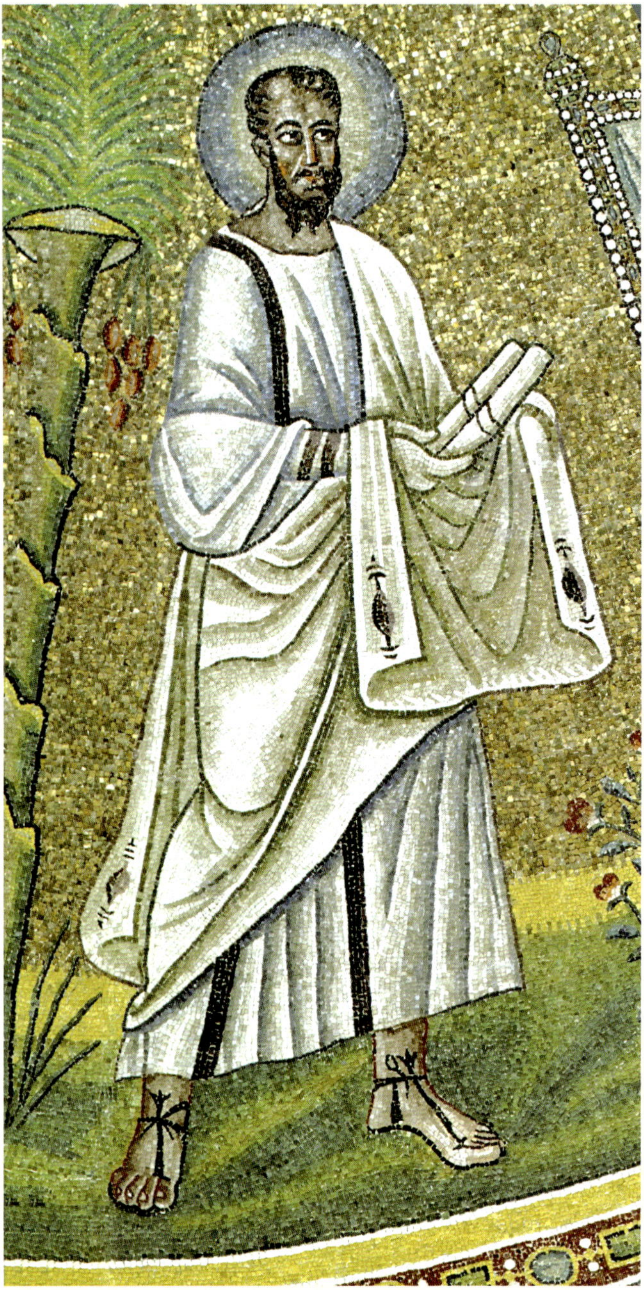

23. ST PAUL
Unknown mosaic artist

23. St Paul

Unknown mosaic artist

Probably the greatest art of early Christianity is in Ravenna. This image of St Paul, to which I am particularly drawn, actually comes, not from Catholic Ravenna, but from the great baptistry erected by the Arians.

Heretics or not, they understood the grandeur of St Paul. It is the typical image, high forehead, dark sideburns, small beard, but the artist expresses a unique sense of movement. This is St Paul perpetually stretching out, passionate to share the Gospel with those who have not the joy of knowing Jesus. He holds scrolls in his hand, either those of the Old Testament or the scrolls of his letters. He holds them as the priest holds the sacred vessels at Mass, they are held within a cloth to express his reverence. Moreover, this is one of the few St Pauls who is moving with determination towards the cross.

Jesus crucified was so central to Paul's thinking that I am always surprised that more artists do not show him looking at or moving toward the crucified Lord. Ironically, the Church had not yet, in the fifth century, come to terms with the physicality of the crucifixion and it is not Jesus on the cross but simply an enthroned cross, no crucifix, that draws St Paul forward. I love the freedom with which he moves, and the grace of his simple garments. This is a minimalist St Paul, but the passion is surely there.

When Paul wrote to the Romans, this is how he introduced himself: "Paul, a servant of Jesus Christ, called to be an Apostle, set apart for the Gospel of God which he promised beforehand through His prophets in the Holy Scriptures, the Gospel concerning His Son who was descended from David according to the flesh and designated Son of God in power according to the Spirit of holiness by his resurrection from the dead, Jesus Christ Our Lord." Paul wants the Romans and all with whom he has contact, (this would, of course, have included the future people of Ravenna, though I am not quite sure about the Arians) to know it was from Jesus that "we have received grace and apostleship to bring about the obedience of faith".

24.
St Paul

by Andrea Di Bartolo (c.1360/70–1428).
Private collection.

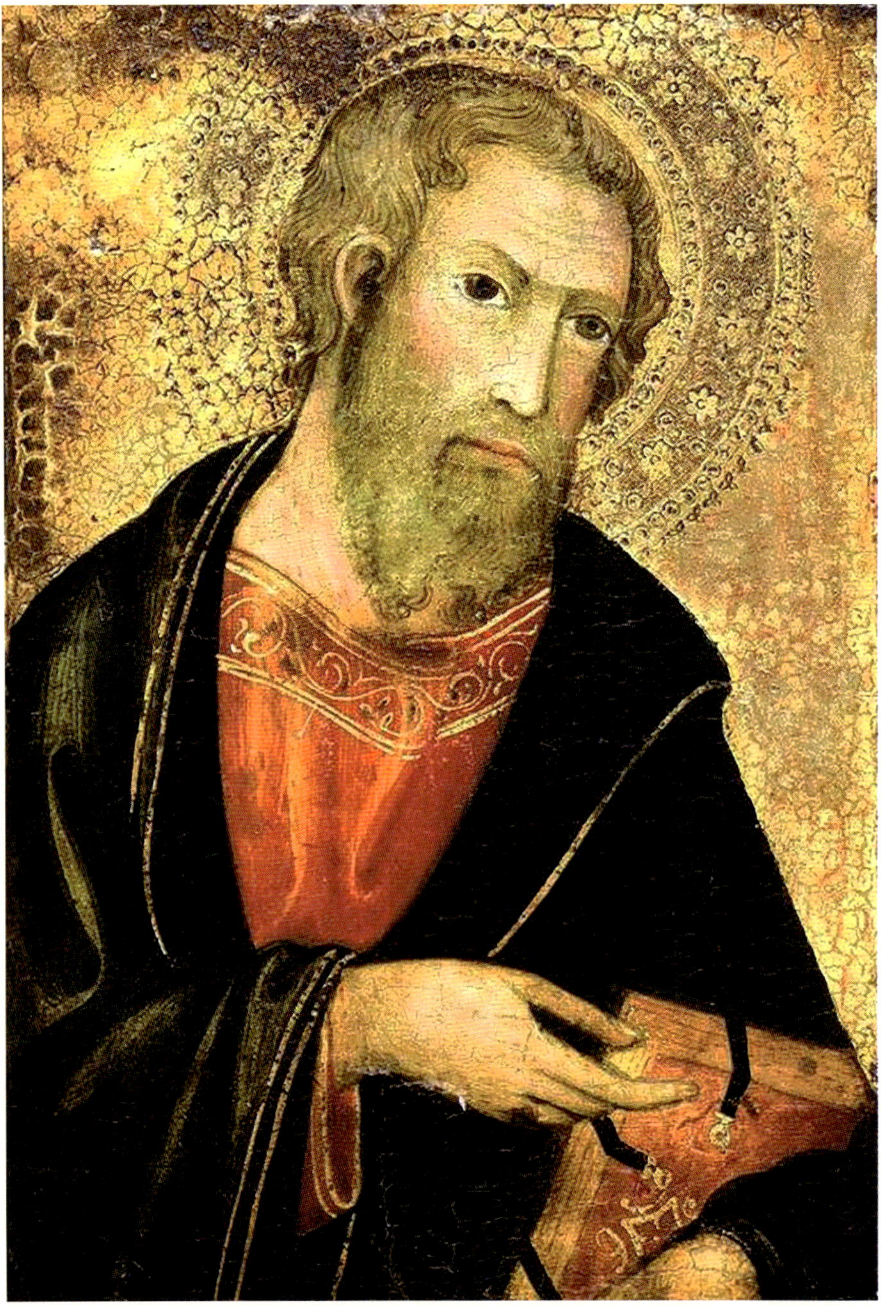

24. ST PAUL
Andrea Di Bartolo

24. St Paul

Andrea Di Bartolo

So many pictures of St Paul show him as stern. It is as if the artists are in awe of the spiritual grandeur of this saint, of his undeviating purpose, of the seriousness with which he sought God. He sought Him and knew, not that he had found Him, but that it was God who did the finding. Many would see the essence of Paul in that powerful sentence "all have sinned and fall short of the glory of God."

Andrea Di Bartolo is not an important artist and this is not an important picture, but I feel it shows another side to St Paul. This is not the stern Apostle of the Gentiles who could call his conscience to witness "that I have great sorrow and unceasing anguish in my heart. For I could wish that I myself were accursed and cut off from Christ for the sake of my brethren, my kinsman by race." No one so loved and esteemed the Jews as this Jew who gave his life to convert the non-Jew. But all that seems far from this gentle, pensive St Paul of Andrea. Even physically he is different, fair hair and pink cheeks, and although he holds his emblematic book, there is no sign of the sword of his martyrdom.

When we read the Acts of the Apostles, it becomes clear how fond people were of Paul, he was loved, and many parted from him with tears. We see this same loveableness in the greetings with which he ends his epistles. "Greet one another with a holy kiss." "My beloved brethren, be steadfast." "It was kind of you to share my trouble… even in Thessalonica you have sent me help once and again… my God will supply every need of yours according to his riches in glory in Christ Jesus." Even the fiery Paul, with his passionate longings that all should understand the meaning of Jesus, had a gentle and affectionate side, which artists rarely portray.

Andrea's St Paul makes one understand how St Paul was able to write with such intimate certainty about love. "Love" he tells us "is patient and kind; love is not jealous or boastful; it is not arrogant or rude. Love does not insist on its own way; it is not irritable or resentful; it does not rejoice at wrong, but rejoices in the right. Love bears all things, believes all things, hopes all things, endures all things." This seems to me to be a face of a man who understands love.

25.
St Paul

by El Greco (1541-1614), c.1600,
Museum of Fine Art, St Louis, U.S.A.

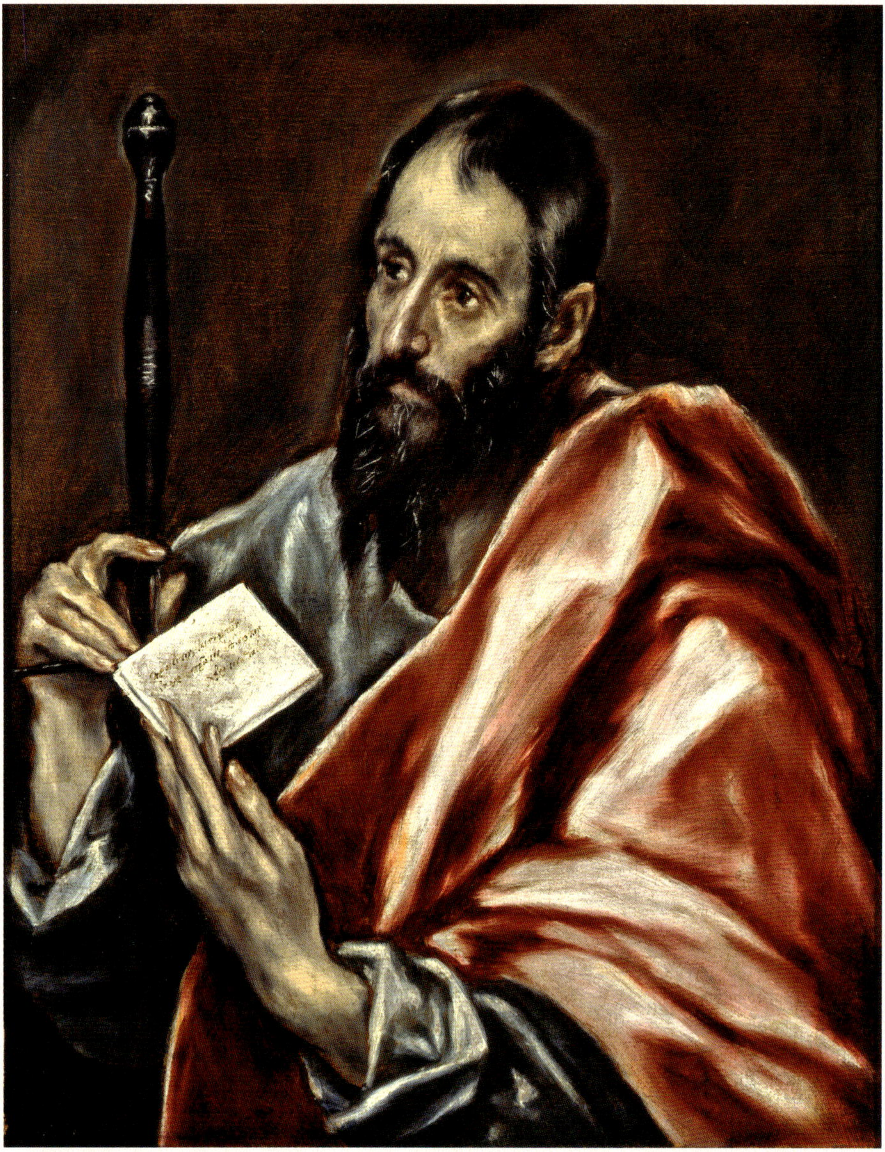

25. St Paul
El Greco

25. St Paul

El Greco

El Greco is one of those artists whom everybody recognises. His figures, in their elongation, seem drawn heavenward, perhaps a lingering heritage of his early days in Crete, as an icon painter. But however innovative and unique El Greco was in his manner, he tended to repeat the matter of his themes. He painted the Apostles (of whom St Paul was always an honorary member) several times, usually showing St Paul as we see him here. One slender hand is draped casually around an elaborate and upstanding sword and the other holds, by his fingertips, a written note.

This is a St Paul afire with dynamic eagerness to communicate Jesus. The great scarlet cloak that hangs loosely around him, seems insecure, as if he were about to move forward and present his note to whomever is standing just outside the picture frame. In the most modest sense, he is stripped for action: there is nothing to hold him back. El Greco, passionate and intense himself, warmed to this intense St Paul, whose desire to spread the Gospel has sunken his cheeks and burnt away his physical frame.

In his letters, St Paul mentions more than once that he is not a man of compelling oratory, and at the heart of his faith is the conviction that it is in human weakness that God reveals His strength. "He said to me, 'my grace is sufficient for you, for my power is made perfect in weakness.'" "I will all the more gladly boast of my weaknesses that the power of Christ may rest upon me… for when I am weak I am strong." This awareness of weakness in oratorical powers was intensified by a consciousness of physical weakness. St Paul speaks of a bodily ailment, and there is also the mysterious "thorn given me in the flesh" which some scholars think might have been epilepsy. But, clearly, what touched the heart of these early converts was Paul's extraordinary personality, that fiery intensity, consumed with love and faith, that so communicated to others the meaning of Jesus. Paul seems to have drawn people to God more by what he was than by what he said. This is surely always the case. We take fire from fire, not from a brilliant theological description of fire.

Encountering St Paul must have been an overwhelming experience. Quite apart from that "intent look" people who had perhaps only the vaguest idea of the wonder of God, were meeting somebody for whom this wonder was his very life "if we live by the Spirit, let us also walk by the Spirit". To meet someone who genuinely and absolutely "lived by the Spirit" is a life-changing experience. El Greco gives us a hint of what this might have been like.

26.
St Paul

by Georges de La Tour (1593-1652), c.1615-1620,
Musée Toulouse-Lautrec, Albi, France.

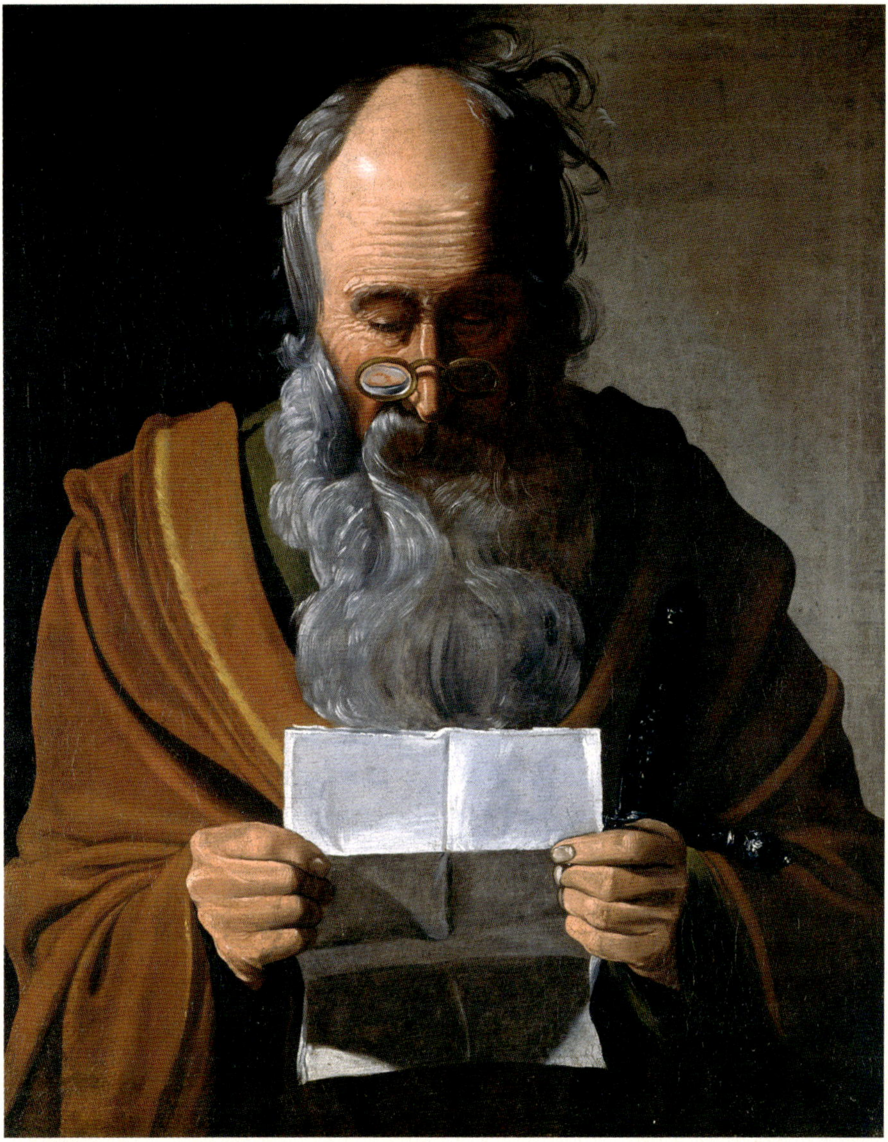

26. ST PAUL
Georges de La Tour

26. St Paul

Georges de La Tour

De La Tour is one of those great artists, Vermeer is another example, who mysteriously fell out of favour, and has now been rediscovered. This extraordinary portrait, in its humanity and realism, shows why he is now so appreciated.

This is an elderly, rather scholarly St Paul, bald head gleaming in the sunlight, intent, not on writing, but on reading. We notice, though, that the sunlight leaves half his face in darkness, and despite the familiarising touch of the glasses, sliding down that long angular nose, this seemingly approachable Apostle is actually a rather mysterious figure. We are aware of the tension with which his hands grasp the letter he is reading, and the intense concentration of those downcast eyes. The Acts of the Apostles show us the dynamic St Paul, journeying, preaching, suffering almost incredible hardships. It is this St Paul we imagine who writes his great letters, always "the giver", far less "the receiver". (As St Paul quotes Jesus as saying, "it is better to give than to receive".) But just as St Paul knew he could only give to others because of what God had given him, ("what have you that you did not receive?"), so St Paul's words to the churches sprang from an awareness of their problems and their needs.

If St Paul did quite a lot of writing, he must have done even more reading and listening. When we go through his letters, we can see how aware he is of the actual state of the Christians in Corinth or Galatia or wherever. De La Tour imagines vividly this power of total concentration, which enables St Paul to grasp the reality of the Christian situation in these distant cities. He is reading without apparent emotion: all his mind is set on understanding. If he cannot enter intellectually and imaginatively into the difficulty of his converts, how can he reveal to them the great Answer the Father has given us in Jesus? "Blessed be the God and Father of Our Lord Jesus Christ, the Father of mercies and the God of all comfort, who comforts us in all our afflictions, that we may be able to comfort those who are in any affliction, with the comfort with which we are comforted by God." St Paul was convinced, "if one member suffers, all suffer together". Of course, there was also a happier side to this: "if one member is honoured, all rejoice together". Mainly, however, the letters he got from his converts and on which he needed thoroughly to concentrate so as to understand every least nuance, dealt with problems. De La Tour's St Paul, homing in on this parchment, seems to be encountering the kind of problem that will shortly require a magisterial and written response.

27.
St Paul

by Tommaso Masaccio (1401-1428), 1426,
Museo Nazionale, Pisa, Italy.

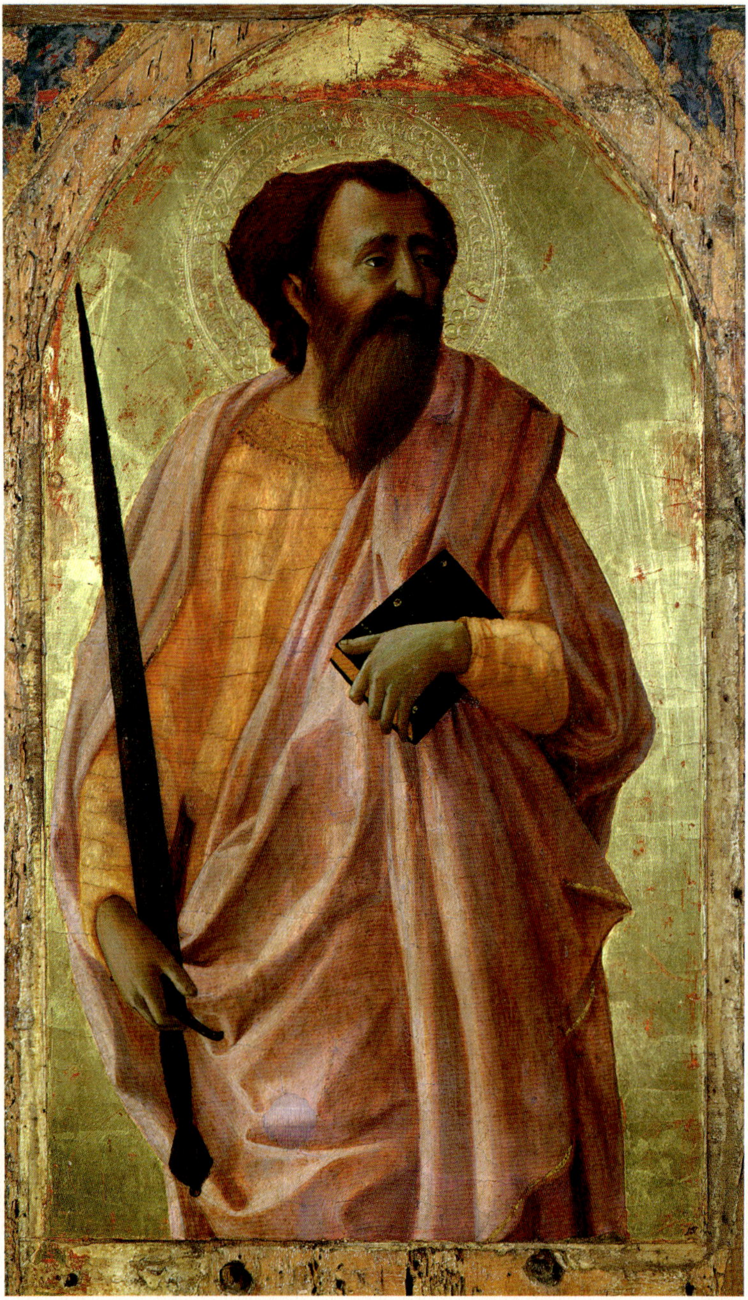

27. ST PAUL
Tommaso Masaccio

27. St Paul

Tommaso Masaccio

Western art could be said to begin with Giotto, but for nearly a hundred years, there was no artist with the capacity to understand his legacy and to build on it. The world had to wait for the fifteenth century and the birth of Masaccio, a genius as towering as Giotto himself. Masaccio died pitiably young, and yet his awareness of the actualities of the body, in three dimensionality and the drama of human existence, has changed the course of art. He is Giotto-come-again. His masterwork is in the Carmelite church in Florence. The Carmelites seemed to have liked him because he also painted a great altarpiece for the Carmelites in Pisa. The altarpiece has long been dismantled and dispersed, and we have little idea of its original appearance but some pieces of it still survive, and this wonderful St Paul is among them. It may be artistic blasphemy, but I am rather glad this St Paul can now be seen isolated, without forming part of a massive altarpiece.

Masaccio seems so to enter into the heroism of St Paul, his moral greatness, that we need to give him our entire attention. He holds the traditional sword and the book, but it is his air of unshakable integrity that makes him memorable. However often St Paul spoke of his weaknesses, it is evident that he was, in fact, one of the greatest of Christian heroes and Masaccio, (whose name is a nickname and means hefty Tom, or Tom the bulky) has homed in on this spiritual heft, St Paul's moral bulk. This is a man of the most profoundly rooted faith, faith that he acknowledges is pure gift. "Therefore, since we are justified by faith, we have peace with God through Our Lord Jesus Christ. Through Him we have obtained access to this grace in which we stand, and we rejoice in our hope of sharing the glory of God." Masaccio sees a saint imperturbable in the "hope": he has no doubt that he and we will share "the glory of God". "More than that, we rejoice in our sufferings, knowing that suffering produces endurance, and endurance produces character, and character produces hope, and hope does not disappoint us, because God's love has been poured into our hearts through the Holy Spirit who has been given to us."

Masaccio is painting "character", not perhaps a genetic character, Paul's inherited nature, but the character of one subsumed by Christian hope. Since he himself was to die so young, one cannot but pray that he could paint such spiritual magnificence because of a response within himself.

28.
St Paul

by Andrei Rublev (1370-1430), 1407,
originally from the Deesis of Zvenigorod Cathedral,
Tretyakov Gallery, Moscow.

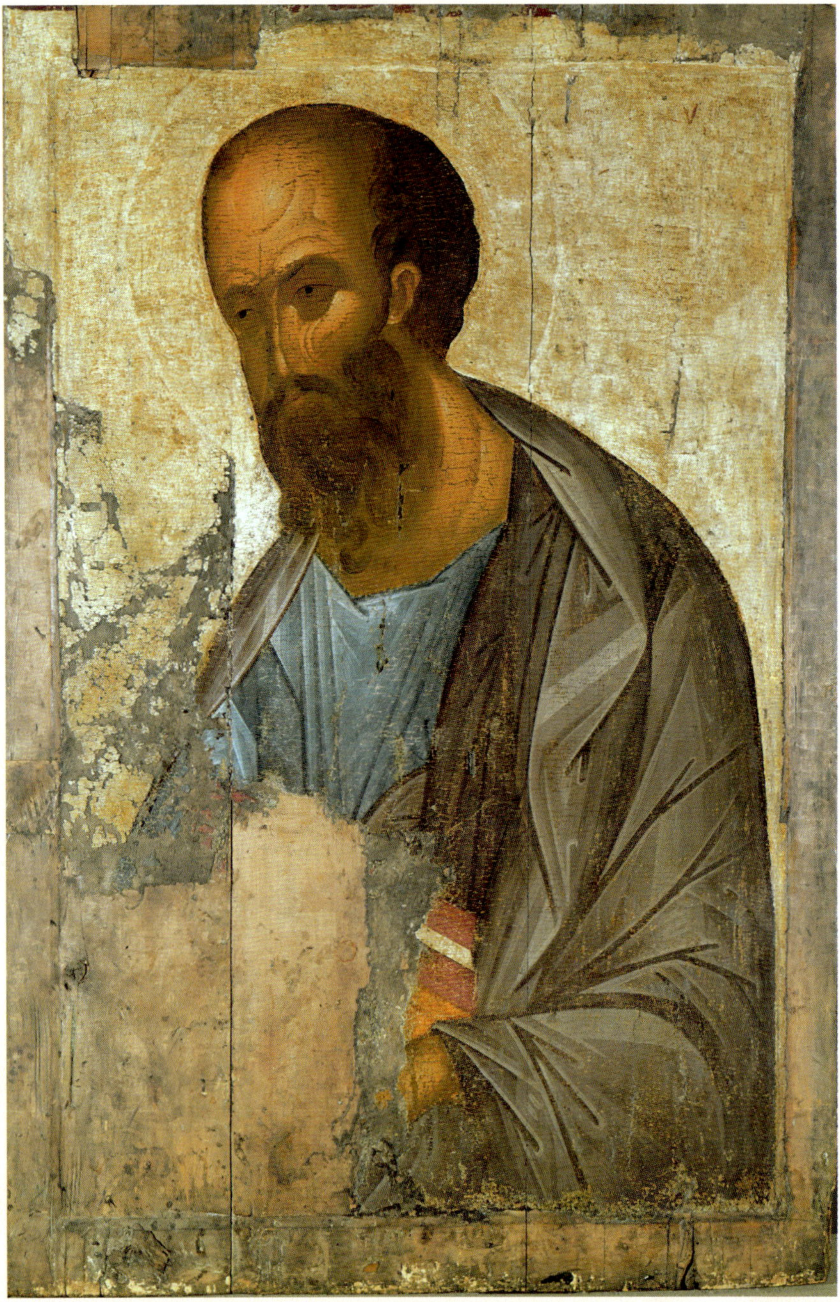

28. ST PAUL
Andrei Rublev

28. St Paul

Andrei Rublev

The Orthodox Church holds icon painting in the most profound esteem. It has been said that in the West their theology has been in books, but in the East, the faith has been presented in the form of icons. Most of these icon painters are unknown, as they themselves would prefer, but there is one name that we all know: that of Andrei Rublev. Moreover, not only was he the greatest of the icon painters but he has been formally acknowledged as a saint, the ideal to which icon painters strove. He was canonised in 1988. Although he seems to have died relatively young, (we do not know his date of birth), he painted at least three images of St Paul, of which this one is the most powerful.

The icon painter was never concerned to make his image "real" to us. It was by definition real: this was the true St Paul. It was the viewer's task to enter into that reality and to become blessed by that golden light in which the saint exists as of right. The icon is damaged, and St Paul may not be holding a sword, but we can see the scarlet and white of his book. Rublev had an astonishing sense of colour and he is drawing us into the heavenly reality of this great Apostle. We notice that his neck seems to be unnaturally swollen, which, in the Orthodox Church, is the traditional manner of indicating the presence of the breath of the Holy Spirit. The saint is himself, but also, more than himself, filled with a divine afflatus. He is lost to all earthly concerns, "pressing forward" to the grace of the sanctifying Lord.

St Paul wrote that "the love of Christ controls us"; Rublev is showing what this means. "Christ died for all, that those who live might live no longer for themselves but for Him who for their sake died and was raised." This is a man unaware of himself, drawn into God, and Rublev desires that we should be drawn with him. All his resources of colour and technique are concentrated on making us aware of that luminous forehead and of the peaceful gaze that communicates so certainly an awareness of the presence of the Risen Christ.

29.
St Paul

by Theophanes the Greek,
originally from the Deesis of Annunciation
Cathedral, Moscow Kremlin, Moscow, Russia.

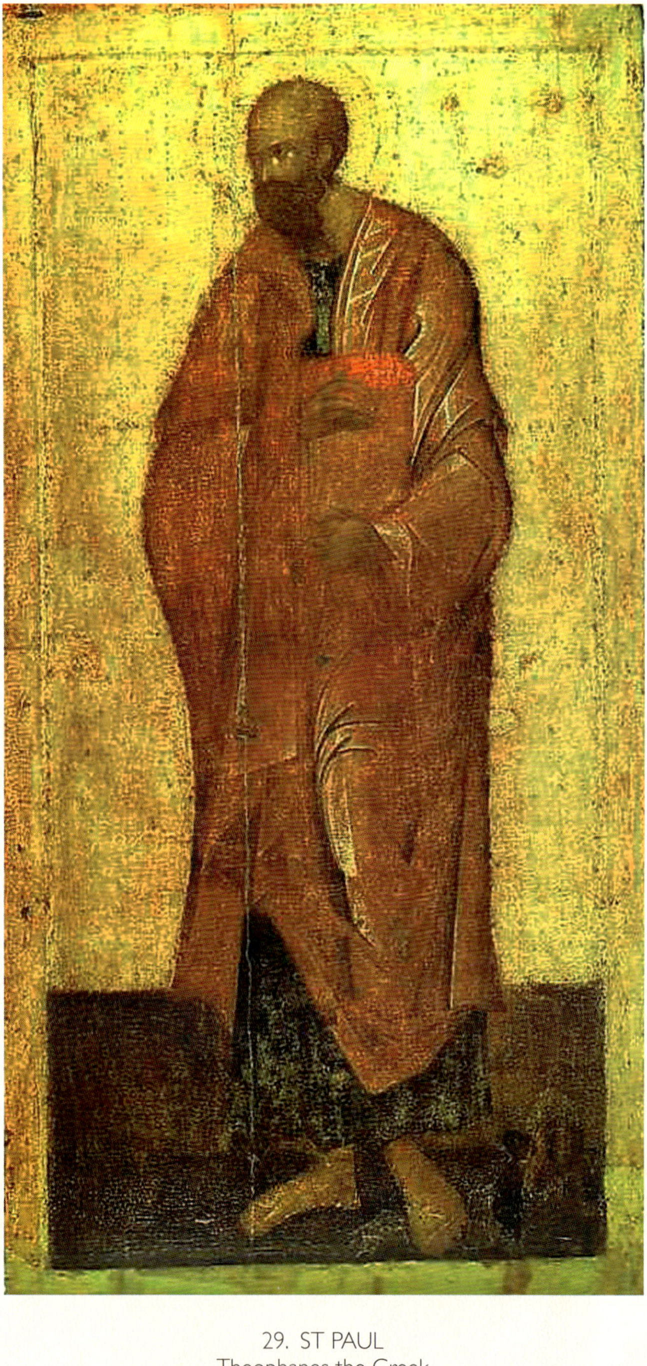

29. ST PAUL
Theophanes the Greek

29. St Paul

Theophanes the Greek

The full title of this icon painter, one of the few whose name has never been forgotten, is the Blessed Theophanes the Greek. The Russians were careful to honour his artistic heritage. He came to Novgorod and then went on to Moscow in 1378, and both his holiness and his insight into the power of art made a great impression on the young Andrei Rublev. Apparently – and here we have one of those rare and priceless quotations – his contemporaries considered him "a most subtle philosopher". Although the ideal of the icon painter was to be so lost in the reality of the image that we are unaware of his own personality, a great artist cannot but reveal himself. This must be what is meant by this praise of Theophanes as both subtle and philosophical.

It is not all that easy, so many centuries later, to read much detail into this icon, but it moves us with its holiness. We see the book, of course, and the bare feet planted firmly on the earth. Yet, what takes our attention is the clarity and brightness of St Paul's eye. We get the unmistakable impression of a man fully alive, completely aware of the eternal dimension, of the God "in whom we live and move and have our being". St Paul wrote to the Corinthians, "we look not to the things that are seen, but to the things that are not seen; for the things that are seen are transient, but the things that are unseen are eternal."

The Blessed Theophanes could only have become "blessed" if he too had lived by an awareness of these things that are "unseen" and "eternal". This invisible world that is so much more real than the world we experience with our senses and yet does not devalue this world but gives it meaning, provides the context in which God can take possession of us. St Paul says, "we walk by faith and not by sight." We realise that the bright eye of this icon seems to see that world of faith and yet not to be ignorant of the world of sight.

St Paul had a great practical understanding of the sanctifying demands of ordinary life. "We are of good courage, and we would rather be away from the body and home with the Lord." (One cannot help thinking that Blessed Theophanes would agree with this "rather be away".) But, if one is to be a saint, like Theophanes, and still more like St Paul, one must continue with: "whether we are home or away, we make it our aim to please Him. For we must all appear before the judgement seat of Christ, so that each one may receive good or evil, according to what he has done in the body."

30.
The Apostle Paul

by Dionysius, (died before 1508), c.1502,
originally from the Deesis in the Church of the
Nativity of the Virgin, in the Ferapontov Monastery.

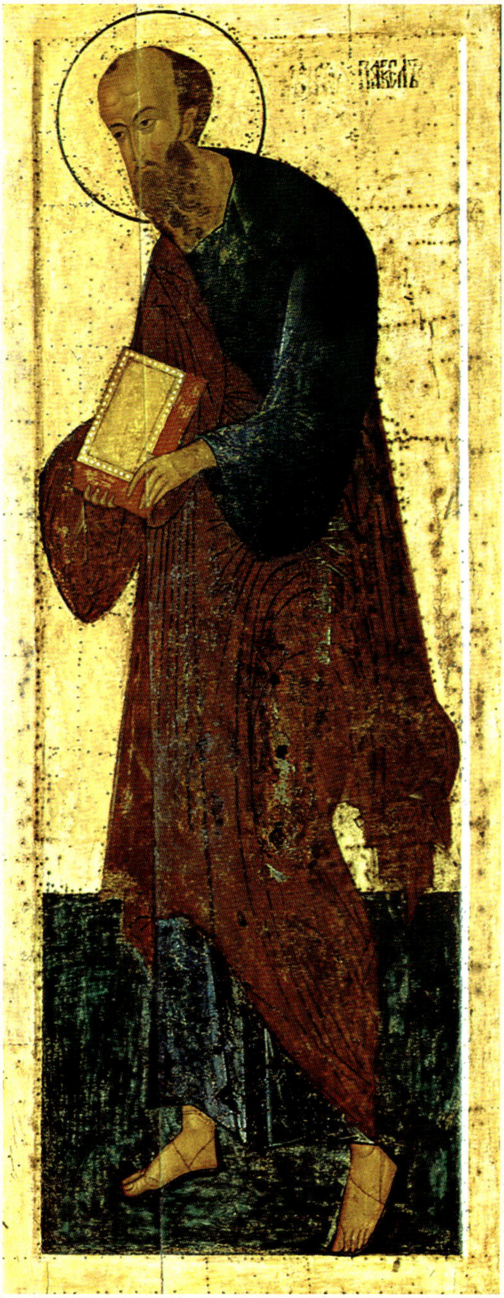

30. THE APOSTLE PAUL
Dionysius

30. The Apostle Paul

Dionysius

Dionysius is the third of the great late mid-medieval icon painters in Russia. In the fourteenth century, the Orthodox Church began to decorate with icons the wall that separated the nave from the sanctuary. It was highly formalised, with icons arranged in tiers, according to strict theological rules. The second tier from the bottom surrounded the figure of Christ with Our Lady to the left and St John the Baptist to the right. Beyond Our Lady was the Archangel Michael and the Apostle Peter, while beyond St John the Baptist was the Archangel Gabriel and the Apostle Paul. This, then, is an image that Dionysius would have painted many times, always seeking to draw the viewer more deeply into the holy reality of the saint. I use the word "viewer" but it was taken for granted that those who viewed, prayed. Some Orthodox theologians hold that one cannot actually see an icon unless one is in a state of grace.

We are looking, not so much at a body, at a figure, as at a revelation of God. Perhaps a relevant observation in St Paul, referring "to the light of the knowledge of the glory of God", which is a treasure that is given us, is that "we have this treasure in earthen vessels, to show that the transcendent power belongs to God and not to us". Even the humble bend of St Paul's body, and the modesty with which he presents his book, seem to speak of this transcendence. St Paul does not stand before the faithful as having any importance of his own, but as being among those who are "heirs of God and fellow heirs of Christ." It was this status of being "fellow heirs with Christ" that so possessed St Paul's being "for all those who are lead by the Spirit of God are sons of God. For you didn't receive the spirit of slavery to fall back into fear, but you have received the spirit of sonship." Far from "falling back", St Paul leans gently forward receiving that blessed Spirit.

The Gospels reverently record how Jesus addressed God as "Abba!, Father!" We can hear the wonder in Paul's voice when he tells the Romans, "when we cry Abba, Father, it is the Spirit Himself bearing witness with our spirit that we are children of God." Because this is a true icon and not merely a religious painting, Dionysius makes us conscious of that Spirit, so plentifully given to St Paul, and as much as we want it, to us.

31.
The Virgin and Child with Saints Paul and Jerome

by Bartolomeo Vivarini, (c.1432 – after 1499),
c.1460s,
National Gallery, London.

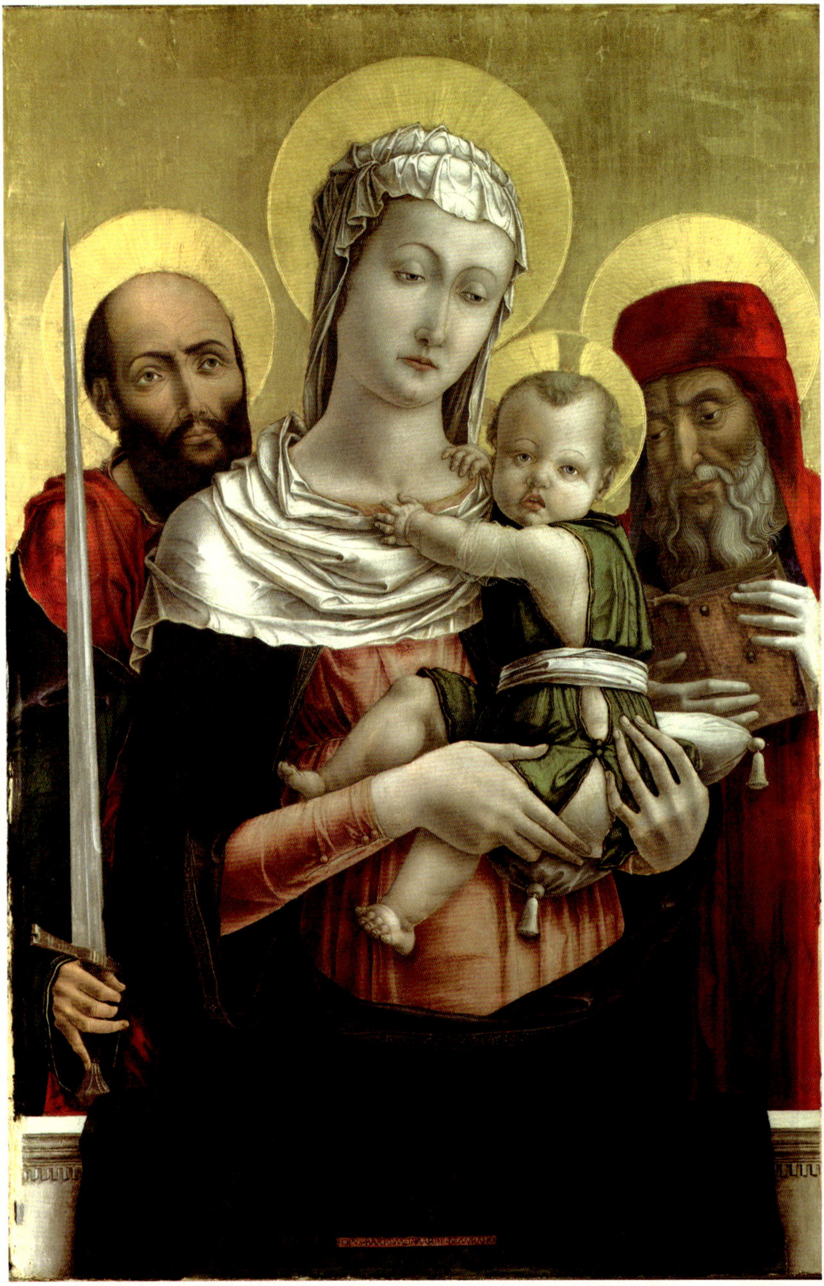

31. THE VIRGIN AND CHILD WITH SAINTS PAUL AND JEROME
Bartolomeo Vivarini

31. The Virgin and Child with Saints Paul and Jerome

Bartolomeo Vivarini

This charming painting of a thoughtful Madonna with her affectionate child, would be more appealing were the composition not so cramped. Squeezed in behind Our Lady are saints Paul and Jerome, both major ecclesiastical figures, who usually occupy a more considered place in the artist's composition. Here they seem to be an afterthought, and I would surmise that St Jerome, intent on his book, is representing the comtemplative life, while St Paul, holding aloft his sword, represents the active life. Yet, St Jerome seems to be above all a scholar, a student of the scriptures, their indefatigable translator, rather than essentially a contemplative. It is St Paul, however heroic his labours, who comes across in his writings as a man of prayer.

It is not only that he continually exhorts his readers to pray, telling them to "pray without ceasing: we ought always to pray and never to faint." I am not even thinking of that sublime passage where he speaks about being caught up into the heavens. What comes through very clearly is Paul's own profound relationship with God, a silent relationship, that made it possible to feel "for me to live is Christ." Only a man of deep prayer could speak about finding himself "not knowing what to pray," and then being aware of the Spirit "speaking within us, with signs too deep for words." It was that communion with God that needed no words that reveals to us the intensity of St Paul's prayer. Even more, it is his conviction that it is not he who prays, but the Spirit who prays within him. Every saint longs to live by the Spirit of Jesus, to be "in Christ": that is what makes them saints. But St Paul had the extraordinary gift, far more than the literary St Jerome, of being able to express this longing and share it with us. All his apostolic zeal had as its aim not merely to teach people about Jesus but to draw them into a relationship with Him. He knew for himself what it meant to "put on the Lord Jesus," "to have the mind of Christ," and he felt his life had no other meaning but to try and draw others into the glory of that relationship.

However, all preachers, in St Paul's time as in ours, have to combat the tendency of their congregations to become over interested in the giver of the message, rather than in the message itself. We see it in St Paul's letters, trying to persuade people to listen to what is said rather than paying attention to the attractions or defects of the sayer. Paul himself was so dynamic a personality that he must have found this a special danger. What appeals to me then, in this painting, is the relative insignificance of the two great saints. But it is a significant insignificance. Paul (and St Jerome) are acting as buttresses to the figures of Mary and Jesus. That is precisely what St Paul wished to do: to bring Jesus into prominence. Of course, the Jesus he preached with such selfless passion was the crucified Christ. Yet, even in babyhood, Jesus bears within him his redemptive future, and the sadness of His Mother's look makes us aware of it. Vivarini depicts St Paul gazing wide-eyed over the Virgin's shoulder, a look of sorrowful resignation on his face, as if he contemplates what is to come.

Those who love Jesus cannot but grieve over His passion, but equally, they cannot but rejoice, to the depth of their being, at His resurrection, which is our resurrection too. None of the New Testament writers, not even St John, is more aware than St Paul of "the mystery of Christ." I can imagine him smiling at this painting, delighted to be squashed into the background, so that Jesus might be "all in all".

32.
St Paul at His Desk

by Tournier or Valentin, c.1618,
Blaffer Foundation Collection.

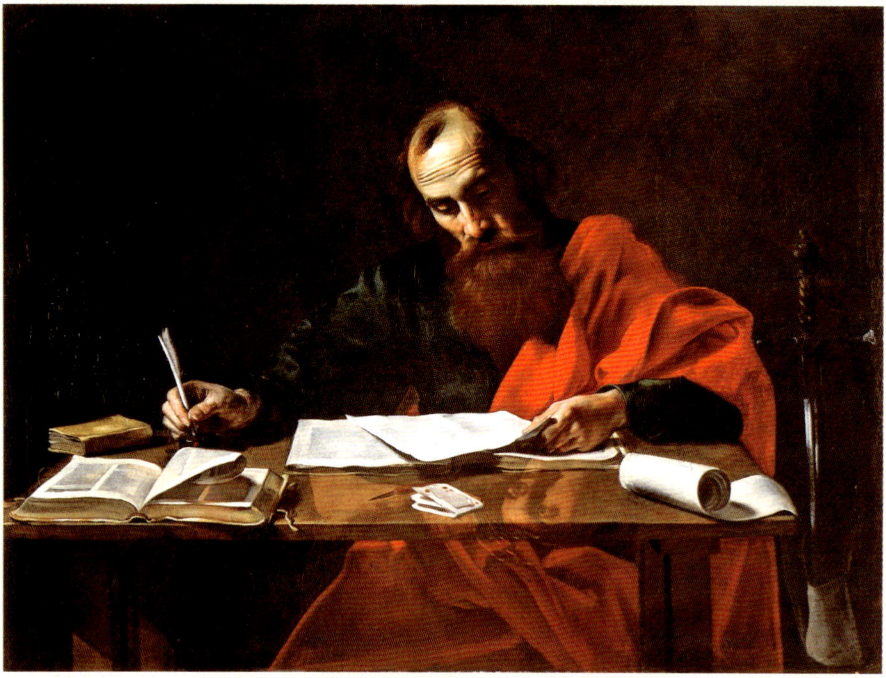

32. ST PAUL AT HIS DESK
Tournier or Valentin

32. St Paul at His Desk

Tournier or Valentin

Both Tournier and Valentin, powerful painters, were drawn to St Paul, that powerful communicator, and this is a very forceful painting which some scholars think is by Tournier and others by his great contemporary Valentin.

Artists seem to have been drawn to the idea of St Paul engaged in the art of composition, but often they show him at the end of his life: this is an imprisoned St Paul, wearily struggling to stretch out to his converts. This picture, though, shows a St Paul still free and still vigorous. Tournier was no historian and he was blithely unconcerned about anachronism: little here is historically accurate. The Bible, which St Paul is consulting, one page still bent over from his search for the exact quotation, did not exist in this form until many years later. St Paul would never have handled an actual 'book.' In fact, scholars think that it was the need to possess the New Testament in a more accessible form, that actually hastened the transition from the scroll to the bound book.

It is also highly probable that St Paul dictated all his letters, writing them indeed, but not with his own hand. (His first letter to the Corinthians authenticates itself, by adding, at the very end, "I, Paul, write this greeting in my own hand." Tournier's St Paul is far from merely adding a greeting. He is thinking deeply, pondering how best to convince his hearers of the reality of Jesus and the glorious extent to which he has fulfilled all the promises of the Old Testament. Tournier may not have his facts literally correct, but spiritually he understands St Paul to the heart. This letter writing St Paul, so intent, so serious, reminds us of the tribute St Paul paid his dear Corinthians. "You, yourselves, are our letters of recommendation, written on your hearts, to be known and read by all men; and you show that you are a letter from Christ delivered by us, written not with ink but with the Spirit of the Living God, not on tablets of stone, but on tablets of human hearts."

This picture of the saint, hollow of cheek, wrinkled of forehead, arduously composing his letter, is a visual equivalent of what St Paul says. He himself is, most truly, "a letter of Christ...written not by ink, but by the Spirit of the Living God." The seventeenth century had an interest in the self portrait (this is clearest in Rembrandt but by no means unique to him). In a way, Tournier maybe showing us a different kind of 'self protrait', the Christ portrait, that St Paul offers us in all his letters. "I live, no, not I, it is Christ who lives in me." Perhaps we should advert to the solid darkness of the background, suggesting both St Paul's isolation and the spiritual, non-earthly significance of the light that plays so brightly over his face and his writing desk.

33.
St Paul

Attributed to the Master of the Pala Sforzesca
(active c.1495-1520), c.1495,
National Gallery, London.

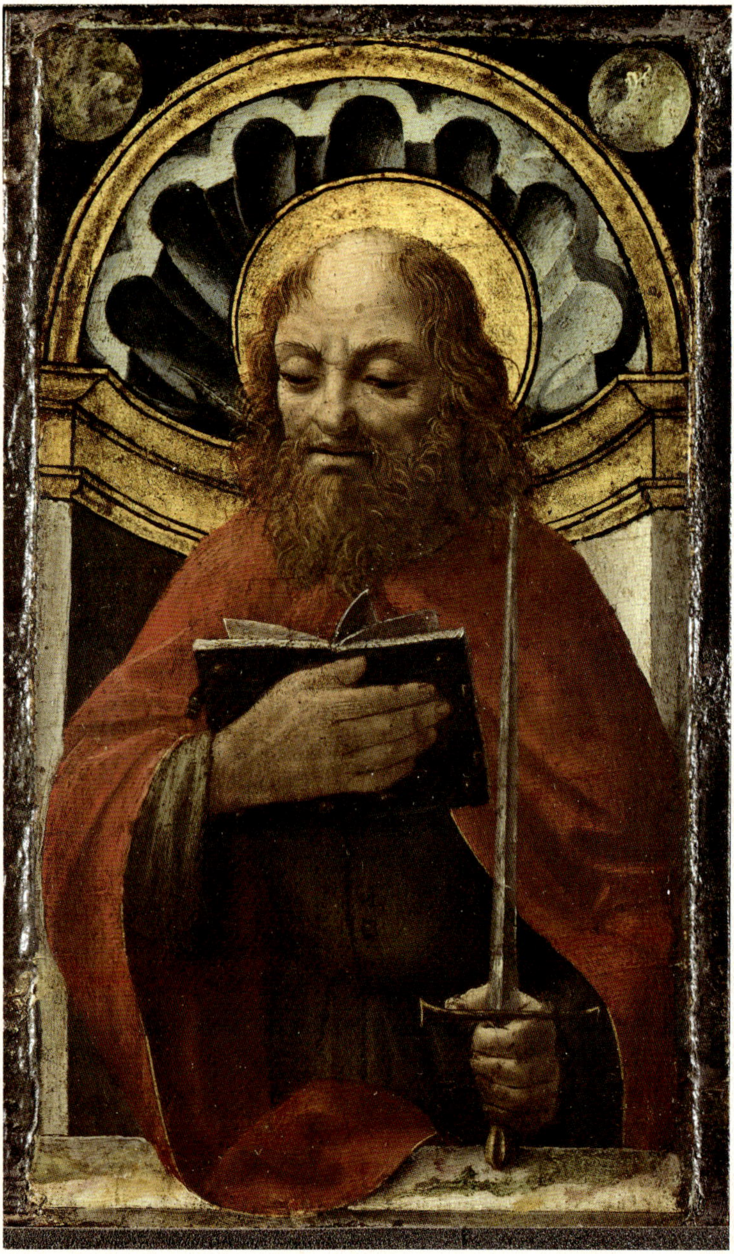

33. ST PAUL
Attributed to the Master of the Pala Sforzesca

33. St Paul

Attributed to the Master of the Pala Sforzesca

When scholars do not know the name of an artist, but do recognise his style, a name can be fabricated. He is called master of his most famous work. The artist who created this impressive St Paul is most famous for a work that is now in one of the great Italian museums, the Brera, in Milan. Almost nothing is known about him, but there is a suggestion that he was influenced by Leonardo DaVinci: the faintly enigmatic smile on St Paul's face does, indeed, have a remote suggestion of the famously mysterious Mona Lisa. Of course, this picture is by no means in that elevated league, but I love it for its gentleness.

St Paul may be holding his sword, but all his attention is on the book, held so close to his eyes that we assume he is short-sighted. He has a very lived-in face, marked by his years of experience. We know he has suffered, but through that suffering he has come to a deep peace. As always with St Paul, it is not "his" peace, but the peace that God gives so freely. "Since we are justified by faith, we have peace with God through our Lord Jesus Christ." It is this happiness within the peace of God that makes St Paul so warm and human a character: not many artists show this but it is the most striking attribute of this particular painting. This is the gentle St Paul who wrote "bless those who persecute you; bless and do not curse them. Rejoice with those who rejoice, weep with those who weep. Live in harmony with one another; do not be haughty, but associate with the lowly; never be conceited." Even the way he clasps his book to his bosom, peering down at it, tells us that this St Paul speaks from the heart when he counsels the Romans never to be 'conceited'.

The very warmth of the colouring here suggests affection "but pay no one evil for evil, but take thought for what is noble in the sight of all." And then St Paul adds that appealing, earthly admonition: "if possible, so far as it depends upon you, live peaceably with all". If we are not "conceited", if we accept that peace is God's gift, then we will have the humility to recognise that we can only act lovingly "so far as it depends" upon ourselves. St Paul's realism is one of his most attractive characteristics. The Master of the Pala Sforzesca is not one of the great artists, and Leonardo would have disdained him, but I think that this small and unusual picture shows a great understanding of St Paul.

34.
St Paul Writing

by Pier Francesco Sacchi (c.1485-1528), 1520s,
National Gallery, London.

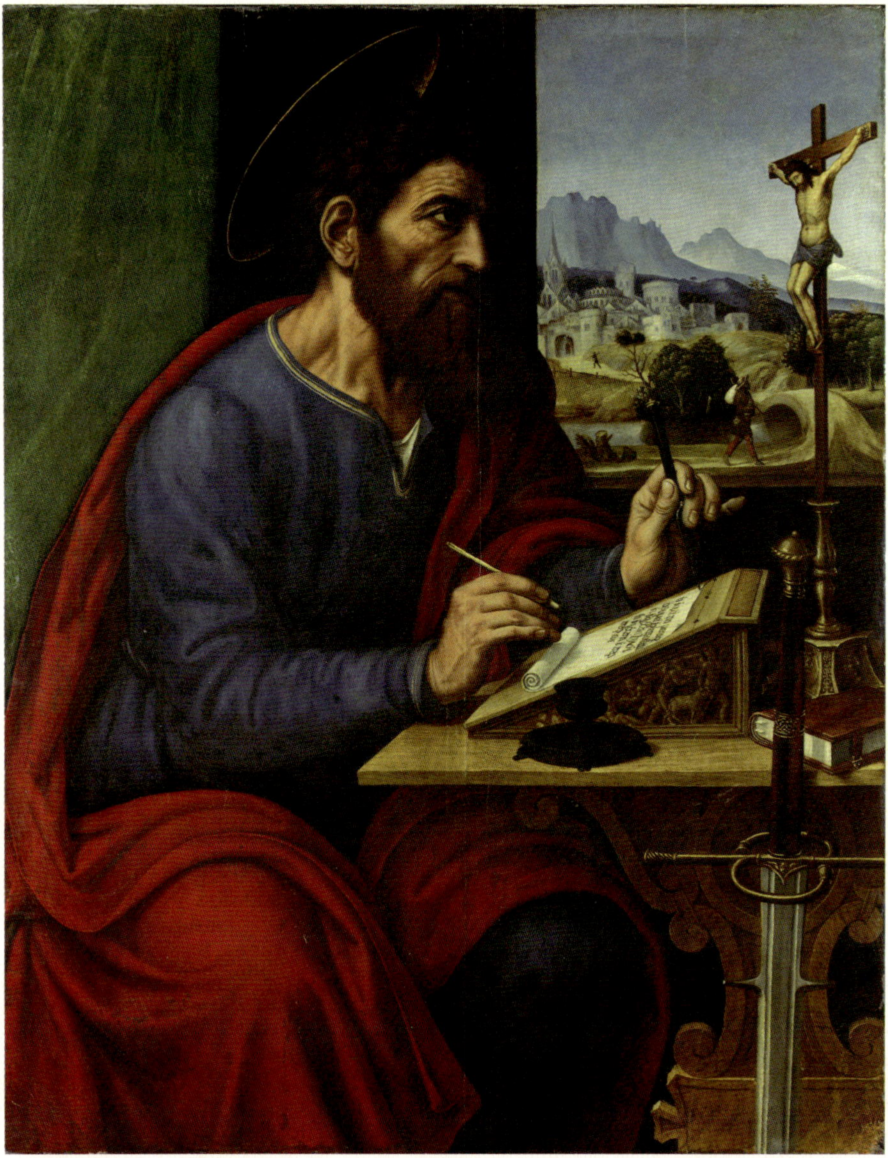

34. ST PAUL WRITING
Pier Francesco Sacchi

34. St Paul Writing

Pier Francesco Sacchi

We know very little about Pier Francesco Sacchi and very few works of his still exist. What surprises me here is that it is one of the very few paintings of St Paul that give prominence to the crucifix. The early church found it very hard to come to terms with the manner in which Jesus died. For us it has been sanitised by time. The cross is the Christian emblem. It crowns our churches, it adorns our altars, we wear it around our necks, we sign ourselves frequently. We find it easy to forget that this death was so horrible that the Romans inflicted it only on slaves and the worst of evil doers.

For centuries the church could barely brings itself to show a cross, let alone Jesus hanging on it. When the great breakthrough is made, Jesus triumphs over the cross, erect and victorious. But St Paul never allowed himself to forget the reality of his redemption: Jesus died for us and he died crucified. "I am not ashamed of the Gospel," he tells us, even though "the word of the cross is folly to those who are perishing, but to us who are being saved it is the power of God." Then St Paul quotes Isaiah, "for it is written, 'I will destroy the wisdom of the wise, and the cleverness of the clever I will thwart.' " St Paul understands to the full that "the wise and the clever" will never be able to understand the cross. "For Jews demand signs and Greeks seek wisdom, but we preach Christ crucified, a stumbling block to Jews and folly to gentiles, but to those who are called, both Jews and Greeks, Christ the power of God and the wisdom of God." It was from this total sacrifice of Jesus, that made no sense except in the terms of radical love, that St Paul came to understand what love could be. Sacchi shows him gazing at the crucifix while he struggles to write about love to the Corinthians. The words on the parchment before him read: "love is patient and kind; love is not jealous or boastful; it is not arrogant or rude." This is the best known passage in all the Epistles and we know how it ends: "so faith, hope, love abide, these three; but the greatest of these is love." Through the window, we see a glimpse of the world and its people, quite indifferent to the sacrifice of Jesus and its redemptive power. But Paul is not indifferent. We can see how he yearns to bring home to us what this death means, and how he himself has his heart firmly fixed on "Jesus Christ, and Him crucified".

35.
An Elderly Man as St Paul

by Rembrandt (1606-1669), c.1659,
National Gallery, London.

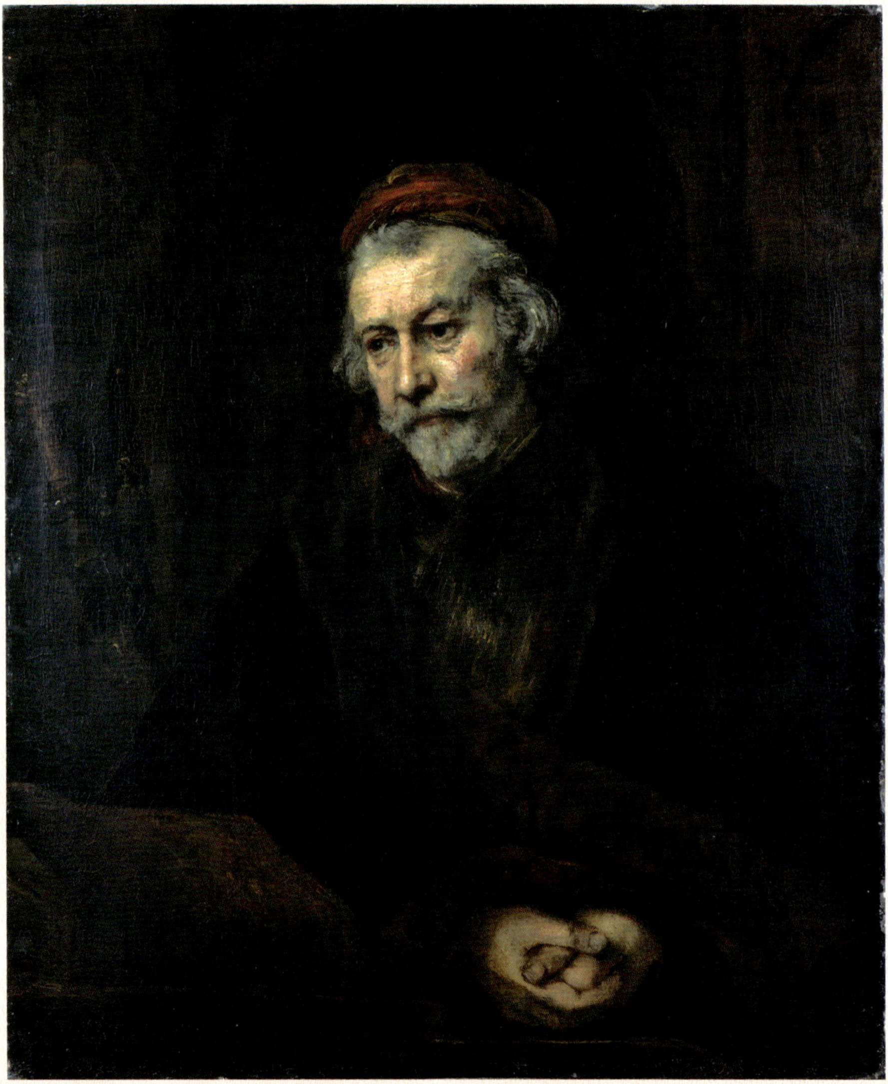

35. AN ELDERLY MAN AS ST PAUL
Rembrandt

35. An Elderly Man as St Paul

Rembrandt

More than once, Rembrandt painted groups of apostles and saints. This picture seems to come from such a group painted when he was on the threshold of his last, great period. It is both a portrait of an elderly man and an image of the saint. Although hard to discern, the sword is there and the book, and yet this is a gentleman very much of Rembrandt's own times. The interest is that Rembrandt could see such a man as a true image of the great apostle. There is no fire here, no sense of apostolic ardour. We cannot imagine this St Paul "arguing day and night in the synagogues". This is an apostle worn out by what he has suffered.

It could be that Rembrandt imagines him thinking back to those early years. "Five times I have received at the hands of the Jews the forty lashes less one. Three times I have been beaten with rods; once I was stoned… on frequent journeys, in danger from rivers, danger from robbers, danger from my own people, danger from gentiles, danger in the city, danger in the wilderness, danger at sea, danger from false brethren." All these dangers are in the past but they have left an indelible mark. Not only have they tired out St Paul's body, (look at those sunken eyes and the feverish flush on his cheek) but they have worn out the exuberance of his spirit. It is not, no, never, that he regrets what he has suffered for the sake of Christ my Lord "I have suffered the loss of all things, and count them as refuse, in order that I may gain Christ and be found in Him, not having a righteousness of my own, based on law, but that which is in faith in Christ, the righteousness from God that depends on Faith."

No artist has so understood the human heart as has Rembrandt, and he seems to have a special insight into the heart of the elderly. His own portraits of his ageing self are breathtaking. Here he sees an ageing St Paul, battered, but not broken, silently at peace in the grace of his Lord. If we see sadness here, it is surely the redemptive sadness of one who understands that most often those to whom he preached, rejected the word of God. He must have been very conscious of the "many, of whom I have often told you and now tell you even with tears, live as enemies of the cross of Christ." For someone so aware of the free grace given in Jesus, the indifference of these multitudes must have been a constant and intolerable grief.

36.
St Paul Seated Reading

After Jacob de Gheyn III (c.1596-1641), c.1620,
National Gallery, London.

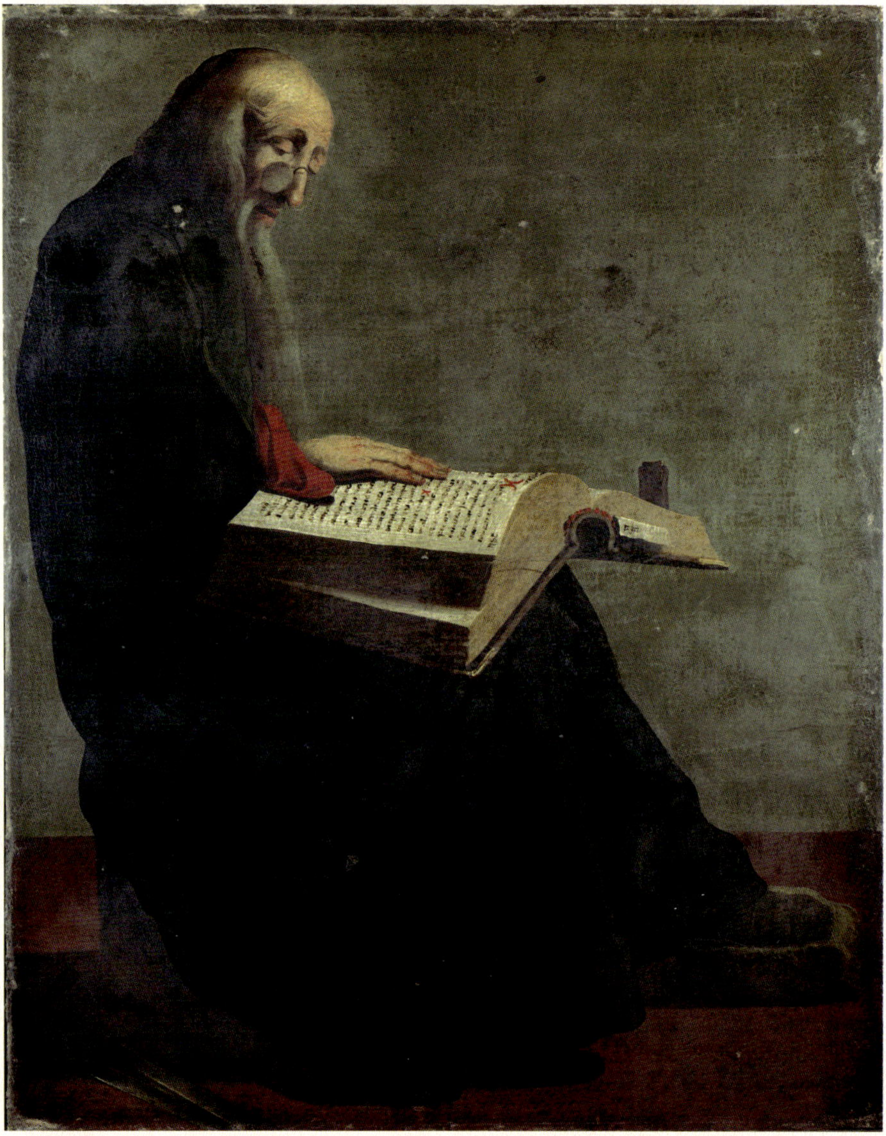

36. ST PAUL SEATED READING
After Jacob de Gheyn III

36. St Paul Seated Reading

After Jacob de Gheyn III

Jacob de Gheyn III is hardly a household name, and there are very few paintings of his, although he left more than a hundred drawings. Some unknown artist painted this St Paul from the de Gheyn's etching, and it is an image well worth the preservation.

We notice that the sword is laid very inconspicuously on the floor behind him and that this elderly scholar is wrapped in the study of the Old Testament. There are really only two centres of interest, St Paul's magnificently domed head, and the extraordinarily massive book, which he balances with difficulty upon an elderly knee. We can deduce perhaps, that this is a St Paul in prison: when else would he have time and leisure for such an absorbed study of the scriptures? This is a wonderful depiction of the sustenance we can draw from the faithful study of the word of God.

Thinking about the Old Testament St Paul bursts out in rapture: "Oh the depth of the riches and wisdom of the knowledge of God! How unsearchable are His judgements and how inscrutable His ways!" As so often with St Paul, it is the words of Isaiah that are inspiring him "for who has known the mind of the Lord, or who has been his counsellor?" He dwells lovingly too on the mysterious book of Job: "or who has given a gift to Him that He might be repaid?" We can imagine this St Paul murmuring to himself what he has written to the Romans: "for from Him and through Him and to Him are all things. To Him be glory for ever. Amen." For St Paul, 'amen' which we say so easily, whether reading it in his letters or as an habitual element in our liturgy, had a mystical significance. He reveals this as he is writing his Second Letter to the Corinthians. They have been upset – critical, in fact – because they had expected him to visit them and he had not turned up. In trying to explain why it had been impossible, he launches into the wonderful passage that ends with his personal understanding of the word "Amen". "Do I make my plans like a worldly man, ready to say Yes and No? As surely as God is faithful, my word to you has not been Yes and No. For the Son of God, Jesus Christ, whom we preached among you, Silvanus and Timothy and I, was not Yes and No; but in Him it is always Yes. For all the promises of God find their Yes in Him. That is why we utter the Amen through Him to the glory of God." Of all that St Paul wrote, this is my favourite line, that "in Him it is always Yes", always "Amen", always "so be it". He says the Amen for us and in us, Jesus is our Yes.

37.
Saints Peter and Paul

by Carlo Crivelli (c.1435 – c.1494), c.1470s,
National Gallery, London.

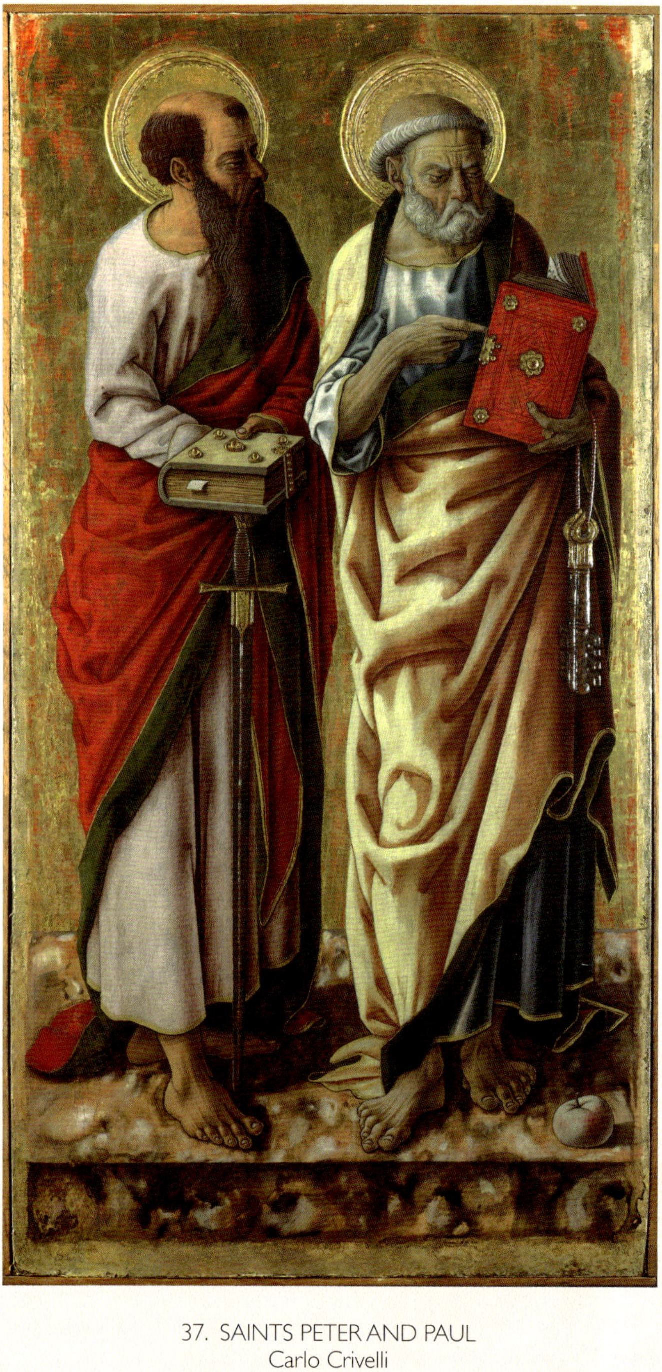

37. SAINTS PETER AND PAUL
Carlo Crivelli

37. Saints Peter and Paul

Carlo Crivelli

Carlo Crivelli is a distinctive artist. All he paints is hard edged, sharply outlined. It is as if his bodies are hewn from the rock, and the fruit which so often decorates his work (see the apple on the lower right) is carved from marble. This makes for compelling and sometimes disturbing pictures.

There is certainly an element of disturbance here, if we look at the tense veins in St Peter's hand or the swollen joints of the apostles' feet. What I find so enthralling here though, is a rare touch of comedy. When we read the Acts of the Apostles, we are told how the church developed from its Jewish origins and, with difficulty, came to terms with them. The apostles in Jerusalem were disturbed by the freedom with which St Paul had been baptising the non-circumcised gentiles. Christianity was the predestined development of Judaism, its fulfilment. Which elements of the original covenant were to be preserved and which had lost their force after the redemptive sacrifice of Jesus?

This was a legitimate area of concern and St Luke gives it full weight. There is a so-called "Council of Jerusalem" and an agenda is agreed, the most important item being the non-necessity of circumcision. In St Luke's account all is sweetness and light, Peter and Paul embrace. However, when we read St Paul's letters, we realise that this peaceable agreement is an oversimplification. All would indeed come right, and Peter and Paul, equally sanctified, would both be martyred in the holy city. In the meantime though, there were difficulties. St Paul minces no words when he writes to the Galatians. "When Cephas (Peter) came to Antioch I opposed him to his face, because he stood condemned… fearing the circumcision party. And with him, the rest of the Jews acted insincerely… but when I saw that they were not straightforward about the truth of the Gospel, I said to Cephas before them all 'if you, though a Jew, live like a gentile and not like a Jew, how can you compel the gentiles to live like Jews?'"

We can imagine St Peter accepting the rebuff and acknowledging the truth of it. How could St Peter, that great lover of Jesus, not warm to a man who can say "I have been crucified with Christ; it is no longer I who live, but Christ who lives in me; and the life I now live in the flesh I live by faith in the Son of God, who loved me and gave Himself for me."

Crivelli offers us a delightful vignette of these two great apostles, not quite at odds with each other, but not wholly in sympathy either. St Peter is rather distractedly searching for a proof in his bible, while St Paul awaits his vindication. They loved each other and worked together for the glory of God, but they were not kindred spirits.

38.
The Virgin and Child with St Peter and St Paul

Workshop of Dirk Bouts (1410-1475), c.1460s,
National Gallery, London.

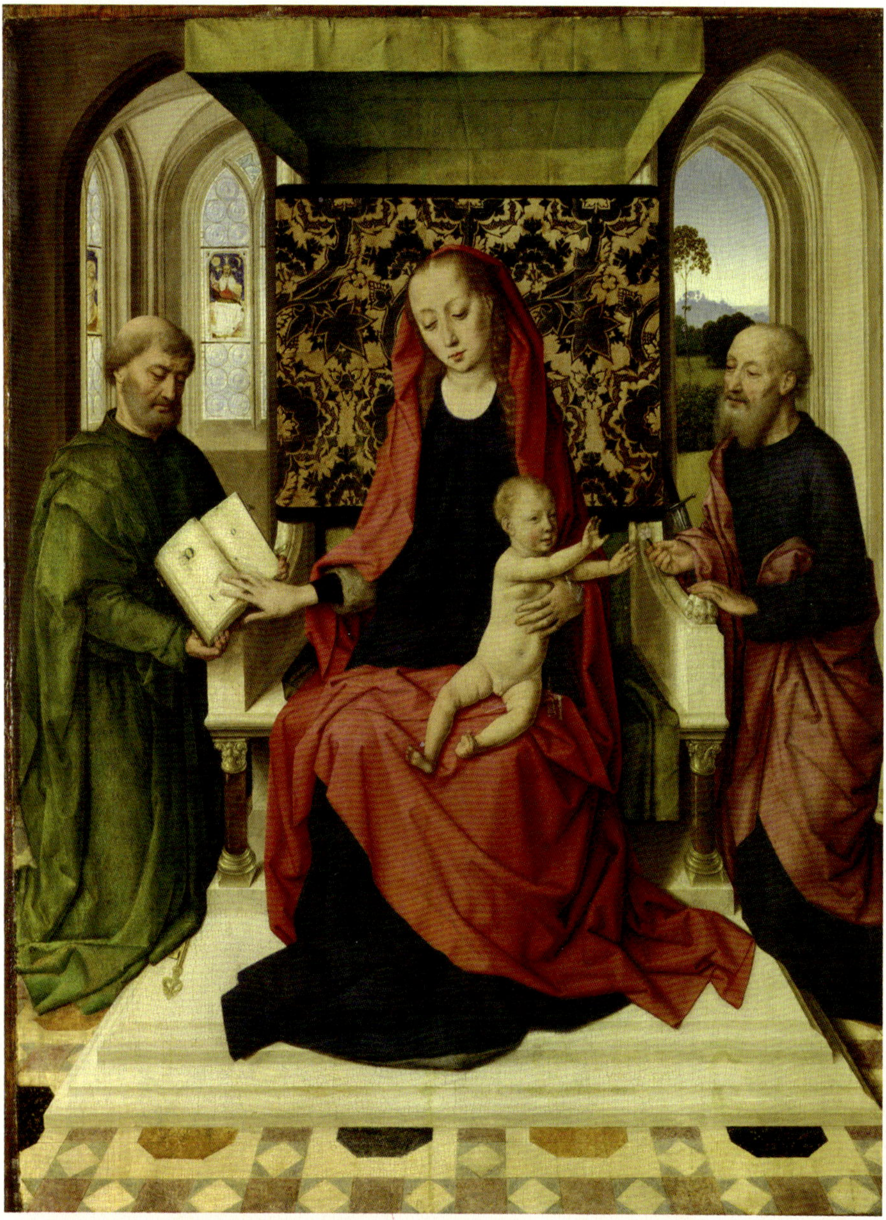

38. THE VIRGIN AND CHILD WITH ST PETER AND ST PAUL
Workshop of Dirk Bouts

38. The Virgin and Child with St Peter and St Paul

Workshop of Dirk Bouts

In what we might call "group pictures" of the saints, St Peter is frequently included, St Paul less so. But this tender little painting shows them both, united by their common love for Jesus. Neither, of course, would have known the child Jesus. He was a young adult when he called St Peter from his fishing to make him "a fisher of men", and he was crucified, risen and ascended to heaven when he appeared miraculously to St Paul. The sheer unlikelihood of this encounter with a child Jesus and his young mother adds a particular poignancy to their interrelationships.

We notice that St Peter has tucked his papal key inconspicuously on the floor beneath his tunic, and St Paul has propped his sword well out of the way against the far wall. It may be significant that behind St Peter is an anachronistic ecclesiastical setting with a stained glass window of Christ enthroned, while behind St Paul, the mighty traveller, is an open window showing a vista of landscape, wood and meadow and mountain. Our Blessed Lady turns to St Peter, who is holding up for her what could be the New Testament or, perhaps, given the medieval date, a Book of Hours (this was a condensed version of the full Divine Office sung by the monks and nuns, making it possible for the ordinary believer to join with them in prayer at every third hour of the day).

St Paul, though, has the privilege of attention from the child Jesus Himself. The little one stretches out his arms, eager to grasp the flower that St Paul so sweetly dangles before Him. Yes, but that flower is a carnation, always a symbol of the Passion. The delight on St Paul's face, as he plays with the holy Child, suggests that he may not be aware of this dark significance, but there is a look on the face of the infant Jesus that indicating that He, at least, knows the meaning of carnation and accepts it. "He loved me and delivered Himself for me."

The mature Paul, in real time, not the atemporal time that Bouts imagines, would live by his conviction that Jesus died for us, totally aware of the price He was paying and paying gladly. "While we were helpless, at the right time Christ died for the ungodly... God shows his love for us in that while we were yet sinners, Christ died for us." We remember from the Gospels that Jesus died rejoicing that "it is consummated". It is done, is it fulfilled. He rejoiced in our redemption. "We also rejoice in God through Our Lord Jesus Christ." In a gentle and subdued manner this picture speaks of that grateful rejoicing.

39.
Twelfth-century Fresco

From the Cappella del Castello Orcau
Museo Nacional d'Art de Catalunya,
Barcelona, Spain.

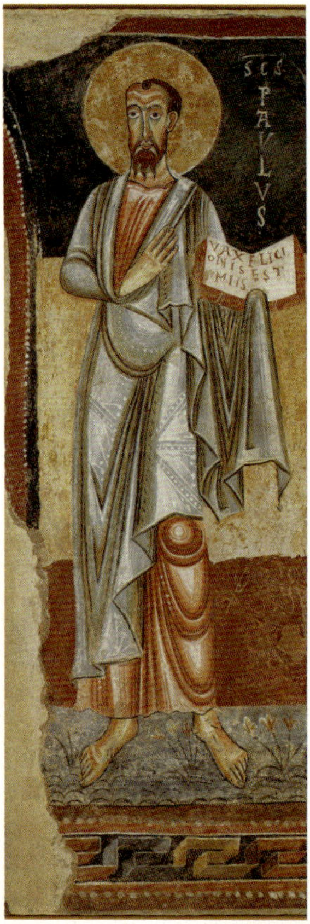

39. TWELFTH-CENTURY FRESCO

39. Twelfth-century Fresco

The long forgotten artist who painted this Spanish St Paul had a unique insight into his complex personality. This is a quizzical St Paul, a man able to stand detached from the busy Vanity Fair of life, and live within the security of his faith. It is a schematic portrayal of a man who escapes the confines of all categories. Notice the minimalist depiction of his three-pronged beard, and that enchanting kiss-curl that still leaves his traditional baldness uncontaminated. What I love here are those large, wondering eyes and the wisdom of that carefully portrayed mouth.

St Paul's natural bent, as we see it at the beginning of the Acts of the Apostles, was to judgement. He judged the early Christians as enemies of God, and it took divine intervention to dislodge his conviction that he knew what was best. Probably, because he always had to struggle against his judgemental nature, St Paul became deeply convinced of our need to accept one another and let God alone be the judge. "You have no excuse, whoever you are, when you judge another; for in passing judgement upon him you condemn yourself, because you, the judge, are doing the very same things. We know the judgement of God rightly falls upon those who do such things." St Paul had come to see that no judgement mattered except that of God. Each of us is a mystery, not only to others, but also to our own selves. It is God who "judges the secrets of men by Christ Jesus".

Quite apart from refusing to judge others, one feels that St Paul had to struggle against resenting the judgement people made of him. It was not that he felt that he was blameless, "wretched man that I am! Who will deliver me from this body of death? Thanks be to God through

Jesus Christ Our Lord!" He had to comfort himself against the pain of human rejection by the certainty that it was only God who mattered. "If God is for us who is against us? He who did not spare his own Son but gave Him up for us all, will He not give us all things with Him?... It is God who justifies; who is to condemn? Is it Jesus Christ, who died, yes, who was raised from the dead, who is at the right hand of God, who intercedes for us."

This St Paul seems to be looking inwards, withdrawing from human judgement, whether given or received and surrendering himself to the only judgement that counts, God's. "Who shall separate us from the love of Christ?" There is a deep interior peace in St Paul who understands that, whatever happens, "we are more than conquerors through Him who loves us." This St Paul is well aware that he is loved.

40.
Statuette of St Paul

Late fourth century.
Discovered in the excavations of the
Christian Cemetery at Cornus, Sardinia,
Museo Archeologico Nazionale, Cagliari, Italy.

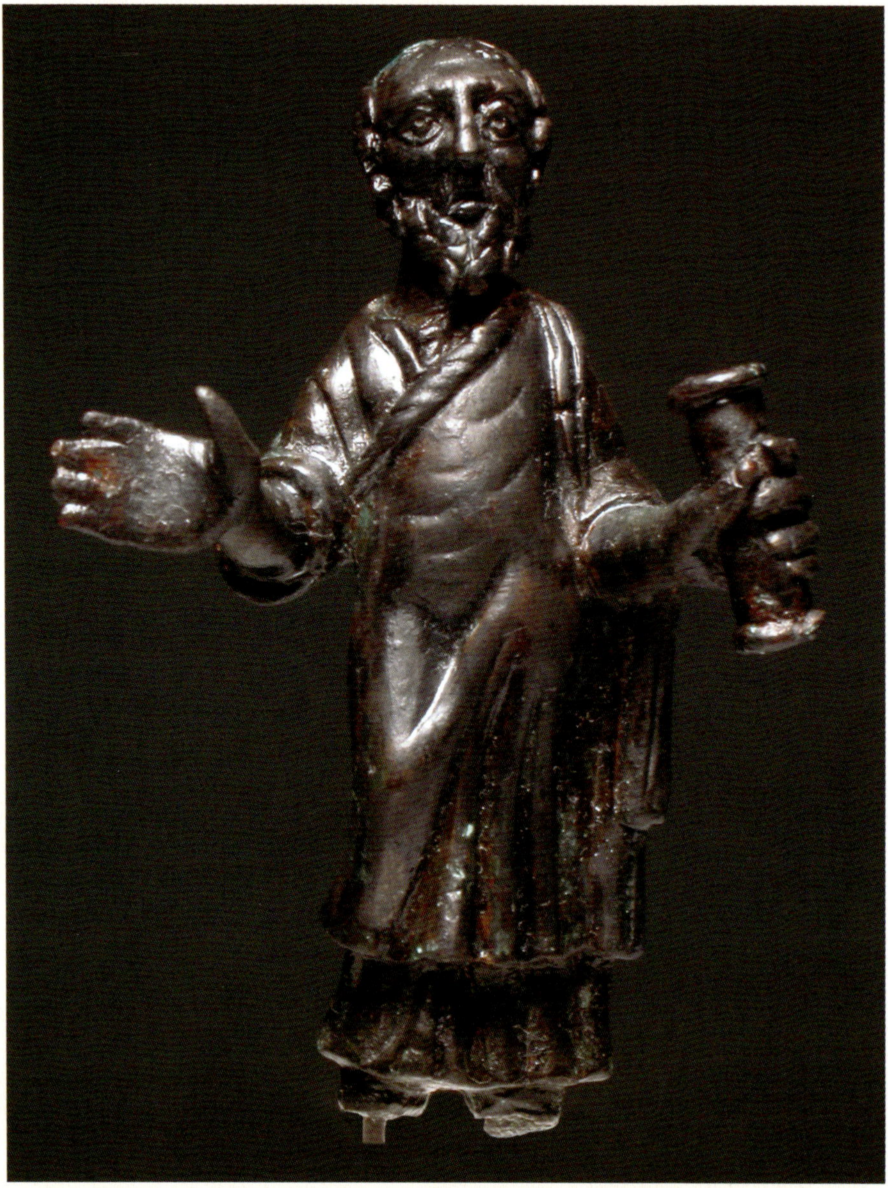

40. STATUETTE OF ST PAUL

40. Statuette of St Paul

In 2007, the Kimbell Museum, in Fort Worth, Texas, offered the public an extraordinary exhibition: Picturing the Bible. All the works it showed were from the very beginning of Christianity with a cut-off point of the early seventh century. There were wonderful things there, suffused with the poetry of those early years in which the infant church tried to understand the riches of God's grace. There were many great works of art in the exhibition, but the one that I loved best and will never forget, was not technically a work of art at all.

The man who made this tiny bronze would have considered himself a craftsman. It seems very likely that this statuette of St Paul was part of the handle of a lamp. Lamps, of course, were essential to life in those distant days. Everybody had one, mostly made of clay, but, in wealthier homes, raised to the dignity of bronze. It would have been a wealthy Christian who bought the bronze lamp of which only the small figure of Paul survives. Whoever fashioned it, or commissioned it, had read the apocryphal Acts of Paul. (Apocryphal means that this text did not make it into the New Testament, and we can take it or leave it as we like.) "And he saw Paul coming, a man small of stature, with a bald head and crooked legs, in a good state of body, with eyebrows meeting and nose somewhat hooked, full of friendliness; for now he appeared like a man, and now he had a face of an angel."

We can decide for ourselves what confidence we put in this description, but at least it has some corroboration in the Acts of the Apostles. When Paul and Barnabas were mistakenly taken as gods, it was Barnabas who was hailed as Zeus the divine chieftain, not Paul. Paul's letters, too, convey the impression that he was not a man of commanding presence, and that it was only the grace of God that marked him out.

Although this may not be a work of art, I find it overpowering in its awareness of Paul's spiritual charisma. There he stands before us, plain, big-nosed, huge hands, nothing physically to recommend him. And yet he blazes with the awareness of God, completely self forgetful, passionately intent on drawing us to the love "of Jesus Christ, and Him crucified". Small, ugly little man as he is, Paul surely has "the face of an angel".

Acknowledgements

Every effort has been made to acknowledge the owner of the copyright material contained in this book. The Publisher would be pleased to hear from any copyright owner who has been omitted or incorrectly acknowledged.

1. *St Paul*
   Andrea Vanni
   1390
   © Museum of Fine Arts, Boston

2. *The Stoning of St Stephen*
   Adam Elsheimer
   1603-1604
   © National Gallery of Scotland

3. *The Conversion of St Paul*
   Caravaggio
   1600-1601
   Santa Maria del Populo, Rome
   © Bridgeman Art Library, London

4. *The Conversion of Saul*
   Pieter Bruegel the Elder
   1567
   © Kunsthistorisches Museum, Vienna

5. *The Conversion of St Paul*
   Francesco Parmigianino
   c.1527
   © Kunsthistorisches Museum, Vienna

6. *Paul Let Down in a Basket*
   Twelfth-century mosaic
   Monreale, Palermo
   © Ancient Art and Architecture Collection, Pinner

7. *The Communion of the Apostles*
   Andrea Bartolo
   © Church of the Holy Cross, Platanistasa, Cyprus

8. *Saul before the Proconsul*
   Raphael
   c.1515-1516
   © Victoria and Albert Museum, London

9. *St Paul Healing the Cripple at Lystra*
   Karel Dujardin
   1663
   © Rijks Museum, Amsterdam

10. *Paul and Barnabas at Lystra*
    Nicolaes Berchem
    1650
    © Musée d'Art, St Etienne, France

11. *St Paul Preaching at Athens*
    Raphael
    c.1513-1514
    © Victoria and Albert Museum, London

12. *St Paul Preaching at Ephesus*
    Eustache Le Sueur
    1649
    © National Gallery, London

13. *St Paul on Malta*
    Adam Elsheimer
    c.1600
    © National Gallery, London

14. *St Paul with the Viper*
    Wall painting in Canterbury Cathedral
    © Angelo Hornak Library, London

15. *Miracles of St Paul*
    Early fifth century ivory diptych
    Bargello
    © Scala Archives, Firenze, Italy

16. *St Paul in Prison*
    Rembrandt
    1627
    © Staatsgalerie, Stuttgart, Germany

17. *St Paul Sends the Letter to the Ephesians*
Miniature from an illuminated manuscript thirteenth century
Biblioteca Marciana, Venice

18. *St Paul*
Aidan Hart
© St John's Bible, Collegeville, U.S.A.

19. Sarcophagus of Junius Bassus
detail c.359 AD
Treasury of St Peter's, Vatican City
© Agenzia Fotografica Luisa Ricciarini

20. *The Beheading of St Paul*
Alessandro Algardi
c.1650
San Paolo Maggiore, Bologna, Italy
© Agenzia Fotografica Luisa Ricciarini

21. *The Ecstasy of St Paul*
Nicholas Poussin
1649-50
Louvre, Paris, France
© Bridgeman Art Library, London

22. *St Paul Enthroned*
Domenico Beccafumi
c. 1515
Museo dell'Opera del Duoma, Siena, Italy
© Agenzia Fotografica Luisa Ricciarini

23. *St Paul*
Unknown artist
Fifth century
Arian Baptistry Ravenna, Italy
© Agenzia Fotografica Luisa Ricciarini

24. *St Paul*
Andrea Di Barbol
Date unknown
Private collection

25. *St Paul*
El Greco
c.1600
Museum of Fine Art, St Louis, U.S.A.
© St Louis Art Museum

26. *St Paul*
Georges de La Tour
c.1615-1620
© Musée Toulouse-Lautrec, Albi, France

27. *St Paul*
Tommaso Masaccio
1426
Museo Nazionale, Pisa, Italy
© Bridgeman Art Library, London

28. *St Paul*
Andrei Rublev
1407
Tretyakov Gallery, Moscow
© Bridgeman Art Library, London

29. *St Paul*
Theophanes the Greek
c.1405
Moscow Kremlin, Moscow, Russia
© Kremlin Museum

30. *The Apostle Paul*
Dionysius
c.1502
Tretyakov Gallery, Moscow, Russia

31. *The Virgin and Child with Saints Paul and Jerome*
Bartolomeo Vivarini
c.1460s
© National Gallery, London

32. *St Paul at His Desk*
Tournier or Valentin
c.1618
© Blaffer Foundation Collection

33. *St Paul*
Attributed to the Master of the Pala Sforzesca
c.1495
© National Gallery, London

34. *St Paul Writing*
Pier Francesco Sacchi
c.1520s
© National Gallery, London

35. *An Elderly Man as St Paul*
Rembrandt
c.1659
© National Gallery, London

36. *St Paul Seated Reading*
After Jacob de Gheyn III
c.1620
© National Gallery, London

37. *Saints Peter and Paul*
Carlo Crivelli
c.1470s
© National Gallery, London

38. *The Virgin and Child with St Peter and St Paul*
Workshop of Dirk Bouts
c.1460s
© National Gallery, London

39. Twelfth-century Fresco
Cappella del Castello Orcau
© Museo d'Art de Catalana, Barcelona, Spain

40. Statuette of St Paul
Fourth century
Museo Archeologico Nazionale, Cagliaria, Italy
© Ministero per i Beni Archeologici della Sardegna, Cagliari